Time I Am -2

Life Is Nothing But Time

Time Is Life, Life Is Time

By
Dr. Sahadeva dasa

B.com., FCA., AICWA., PhD
Chartered Accountant

Soul Science University Press

Readers interested in the subject matter of this
book are invited to correspond with the publisher at:
SoulScienceUniversity@gmail.com   +91 98490 95990
or visit DrDasa.com

First Edition: February 2014

Soul Science University Press expresses its gratitude to the
Bhaktivedanta Book Trust International (BBT), for the use of quotes by
His Divine Grace A.C.Bhaktivedanta Swami Prabhupada.

ISBN 978-93-82947-08-0

Published by:
Dr. Sahadeva dasa for Soul Science University Press

Printed by:
Rainbow Print Pack, Hyderabad

To order a copy write to purnabramhadasa@gmail.com
or buy online: Amazon.com, rlbdeshop.com

Our duration of life is measured, and no one is able to enhance it even by a second against the scheduled time ordained by the supreme will. Such valuable time, especially for the human being, should be cautiously spent because even a second passed away imperceptibly cannot be replaced, even in exchange for thousands of golden coins amassed by hard labor. Every second of human life is meant for making an ultimate solution to the problems of life,
Srila Prabhupada (Srimad Bhagavatam 1.13.17)

By The Same Author

Oil–Final Countdown To A Global Crisis And Its Solutions

End of Modern Civilization And Alternative Future

To Kill Cow Means To End Human Civilization

Cow And Humanity - Made For Each Other

Cows Are Cool - Love 'Em!

Let's Be Friends - A Curious, Calm Cow

Wondrous Glories of Vraja

We Feel Just Like You Do

Tsunami Of Diseases Headed Our Way - Know Your Food Before Time Runs Out

Cow Killing And Beef Export - The Master Plan To Turn India Into A Desert

By 2050

Capitalism Communism And Cowism - A New Economics For The 21st Century

Noble Cow - Munching Grass, Looking Curious And Just Hanging Around

World - Through The Eyes Of Scriptures

To Save Time Is To Lengthen Life

An Inch of Time Can Not Be Bought With A Mile of Gold

Lost Time Is Never Found Again

Spare Us Some Carcasses - An Appeal From The Vultures

Cow Dung - A Down-To- Earth Solution To Global Warming And Climate

Change

Cow Dung For Food Security And Survival of Human Race

(More information on availability on DrDasa.com)

Contents

Preface

Time management is not an instinct, and instead, must be learned. Unfortunately, few schools or parents teach basic time management skills.

Time management is very significant in our present times, even more so than in previous decades. Existing technology allows us to do things faster than before and yet we feel forced to continually increase the pace. As an example, we continue to have difficulty keeping track of the large number of available information even with computers and other gadgets that are extremely powerful. Time management is the component that can give us a sense of control over time so we can quit rushing and loosen up.

Time is an important component of life and so we feel better about our lives when we have the ability to handle our time. Those who are genuinely successful are aware that time management is a crucial skill they have to get good at.

And it's also the most democratic of resources. Every day, every living person is provided with 86,400 seconds. The richest person in the world has just as much as the poorest person, and every day we are presented with the same amount, no more and no less. I am just as rich in time today as the Queen of England, a bum in Bolivia, a student in India, and a factory worker in China.

No amount of money can buy you additional time, and you can't be born into wealth of time. Money can't buy you more time, not even an extra second for millions, nay billions of dollars.

Sahedeva dasa

Dr. Sahadeva dasa
1st March 2014
Secunderabad, India

A Note On The Book Format

This book is based on One Victory A Day™ format. The chapters are arranged date wise. A reader need not read the book serially. He can open any chapter and he will find something useful for the day.

According to surveys, 80% of the books bought don't get read beyond 10% of their contents. They just sit in the shelves. This is especially true in recent times.

The thickness of the book acts as a deterrent, especially due to lack of time. Desperation grows and book lands in the shelf.

In One Victory A Day™ format, the book need not be completed. The idea is to read the chapter related to the day, and then understand, digest, assimilate and implement the information. That is improving life in small measures or changing life one day at a time. Throughout the day, you can try to reflect on and implement the newfound information.

Most of the books bought are not read fully because the reader can not relate the information to his or her life. Purpose of knowledge is not entertainment but betterment of life. Purpose of information is transformation, otherwise it's a waste of time. Ingestion of information without assimilation is like intake of food without digestion.

To scale a highrise, we go up one step at a time. To finish our meal, we eat one morsel at a time. A skyscraper is constructed one brick at a time. And an ocean is nothing but an assembly of many drops. This is the power of small. A big target, when broken down into small steps, becomes easily attainable.

People who are not into reading should cultivate the habit of reading in small installments. Phenomenal achievements can be accomplished by consistent and daily improvements. Good reading is as essential as clean air and water. Anything we do regularly becomes a habit.

The mind's garden will produce whatever we sow in it. Daily we are being bombarded with a massive dose of undesirable information. The only way to counteract it is through assimilation of desirable information.

Time lost

Is Life Lost

Time is the stuff life is made of. Time equals life, and wasting your time means wasting your life. If you spend one hour on someone or something, you are giving away a piece of your life to that someone or something. Therefore you have to be careful to whom or where you give away your life. If you are not careful with time, time just slips away like sand in your fist. Letting time slip away is letting life slip away. Like time and tide, life too waits for none. Life is precious, therefore time is precious.

"Lost wealth may be replaced by industry, lost knowledge by study, lost health by temperance or medicine, but lost time is gone forever", says Samuel Smiles. The same minute never strikes twice

> *Even a moment of one's lifetime could not be returned in exchange for millions of dollars. Therefore one should consider how much loss one suffers if he wastes even a moment of his life for nothing. Living like an animal, not understanding the goal of life, one foolishly thinks that there is no eternity and that his life span of fifty, sixty, or, at the most, one hundred years, is everything. This is the greatest foolishness. Time is eternal, and in the material world one passes through different phases of his eternal life.*
> ~ Srila Prabhupada (Srimad Bhagavatam 6.5.19)

on the clock of fate. Time and words can't be recalled, even if it was only yesterday. You may delay, but time will not.

In this age of rampant consumerism, Thoreau warns us, "The cost of a thing is the amount of what I call life which is required to be exchanged for it, immediately or in the long run." Time is turned into money with which we pay for goods and services. Therefore we pay for things with our life. We don't own things, things own us.

For a moment, try to forget everything you know about working, cashing paychecks, paying taxes, saving for vacation, buying groceries, applying for car loans, and all other matters of financing. Put it all out of your mind, and open your imagination. Pretend that on your eighteenth birthday, you are given a credit card, and you are told, "There is no way for you to check the balance of available credit on this card. You will never know how much money you have available, but whatever that amount may be, it is all the money you will ever have for the rest of your life. You must use only this account to pay for everything from now on. While market conditions may cause the account to collapse without warning, if you are lucky and frugal, you should be able to maintain some sort of lifestyle for the next 60-70 years. Good luck!"

Imagine how that would feel, if you had one account from which you were required to make all purchases for the rest of your life, but you never knew how much money you had, or when it would run out. How would that change your spending habits? What would be different?

For starters, we expect you wouldn't waste a penny of it. You would choose all purchases based on necessity and value. You would allocate funds to purchases for the things you needed to survive, and if you made nonessential purchases (a big screen TV, for example) you would ensure that you got the best deal possible, and that you got the utmost enjoyment possible from the purchase.

Time is the credit card mentioned here. There is only one provided to us and we will never know the balance left in it. We blow it and we blow our life.

Hence laments Shakespeare, "O, call back yesterday, bid time return."

There is a very nice verse in Chanakya niti. You just see how much time was considered as valuable. By this verse, you will know. Canakya Pandita was a great politician. He was sometimes prime minister of the emperor of India. So he says, ayusah ksana eko 'pi na labhya svarna-kotibhih. He says that "A moment's time of your duration of life, moment..." Not to speak of hours and days, but moments. He was considering moment to moment. Just like today, 15th March, 1968, now it is half past seven or past seven, thirty-five. Now this 1968, 7:35, gone, as soon as it is 7:36, you cannot bring back that 1968, 15th March, evening, 7:35, again. Even if you pay millions of dollars, "Please come back again," no, finished. So Chanakya Pandita says that "Time is so valuable that if you pay millions of golden coins, you cannot get back even a moment." What is lost is lost for good. Na cen nirarthakam nitih: "If you such valuable time spoil for nothing, without any profit," na ca hanis tato 'dhika, "just imagine how much you are losing, how greatly you are loser." The thing which you cannot get back by paying millions of dollars, if that is lost for nothing, how much you are losing, just imagine.
~ Srila Prabhupada (Srimad-Bhagavatam 7.6.1 -- San Francisco, March 15, 1968)

Time

Passing Away Imperceptively

We all know time is passing away. The passage of time has been lamented by poets and philosophers. Srila Prabhupada says, "Although everyone knows that the sun is constantly moving in the sky, one cannot normally see the sun moving. Similarly, no one can directly perceive his hair or nails growing, although with the passing of time we perceive the fact of

> The word *gabhira-rayah*, or "imperceptible speed and power," is significant. We observe that by the laws of nature all material things, including our own bodies, gradually disintegrate. Although we can perceive the long-term results of this aging process, we cannot experience the process itself. For example, no one can feel how his hair or fingernails are growing. We perceive the cumulative result of their growth, but from moment to moment we cannot experience it. Similarly, a house gradually decays until it is demolished. From moment to moment we cannot perceive exactly how this is happening, but in the course of longer intervals of time we can actually see the deterioration of the house. In other words, we can experience the results or manifestations of aging and deterioration, but as it is taking place the process itself is imperceptible. This is the wonderful potency of the Supreme Personality of Godhead in His form of time.
> ~ Srila Prabhupada(Srimad Bhagavatam 11.6.15)

growth. Time, the potency of the Lord, is very subtle and powerful and is an insurmountable barrier to fools who are trying to exploit the material creation" (Srimad Bhagavatam 12.4.38).

We know a child is growing, but if you look at it, you can't see the 'process' of growth. After a time period, you only see the 'effect' of growth. Therefore it is said that time is a file that wears and makes no noise.

According to Thomas Carlyle, "The illimitable, silent, never-resting thing called Time, rolling, rushing on, swift, silent, like an all-embracing ocean-tide, on which we and all the universe swim like exhalations, like apparitions which are, and then are not: this is forever very literally a miracle; a thing to strike us dumb, for we have no word to speak about it."

Time's passage is imperceptible. This stealthy escape of time, under my very nose, is often realized too late and too little.

Material birth and death occur within the realm of segmented time. The birth, creation or production of a material object immediately connects it with a segmented sequence of subtle time within the material world. Thus its destruction or death is inevitable. The irresistible force of time moves so subtly that only the most intelligent can perceive it. Just as the candle flame gradually diminishes, as the flowing currents move within the river or as fruits gradually ripen on a tree, the material body is steadily moving toward inevitable death. The temporary body should therefore never be confused with the eternal, unchanging spirit soul.

~ Srila Prabhupada (Srimad Bhagavatam 11.22.44)

How Many Sunday's Do You Have?

Theory of A Thousand Marbles

One man had a busy life, working sixty or seventy hours a week to make ends meet. He was paid alright but he had to be away from his hearth and home.

One day, the gentleman sat down reflecting on his life and did a little arithmetic.

"The average person lives about seventy-five years. Of course, some live more and some live less, but on average, folks live about seventy-five years."

Then, he multiplied 75 times 52 and came up with 3900 which is the number of Sundays that the average person has in his entire lifetime.

He reflected thus, "It took me until I am fifty-five years old to think about all this in any detail", he went on, "and by that time I have lived through over twenty-eight hundred Sundays. If I live to be seventy-five, I only have about a thousand of them left to utilize."

So he went to a toy store and bought every single marble they had. He ended up having to visit three toy stores to round-up 1000 marbles. He took them home and put them inside of a large, clear

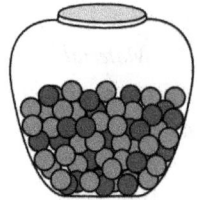

plastic container right in the shack next to his gear. Every Sunday since then, he has taken one marble out and thrown it away.

He found that by watching the marbles diminish, he focused more on the really important things in life. There is nothing like watching your time here on this earth run out to help get your priorities straight."

One fine morning, he took the very last marble out of the container. He figured if he made it until next Sunday then he had been given a little extra time. And the one thing we could all use is a little more time.

Reference:

Dana Anspach

nityada hy anga bhutani
bhavanti na bhavanti ca
kalenalaksya-vegena
suksmatvat tan na drsyate
My dear Uddhava, material bodies are constantly undergoing creation and destruction by the force of time, whose swiftness is imperceptible. But because of the subtle nature of time, no one sees this.
~ Srimad Bhagavatam 11.22.44

Time Management

Be-All And End-All Of Management

You can not care for your life without caring for your time. Out of many different branches of knowledge related to managing life, time management comes first and foremost because time is the background of all our activities and once lost it is lost for ever. Time and tide wait for none. It's the cornerstone to begin a successful and effective life.

Time Management plays a critical part in your life and in your organization. It is even more important than money or finance management. Lost money can be recovered but lost time is gone for good.

It is the number one skill you need to learn if you want to get anywhere in life. Without time management you let yourself over to coincidence. If you study and practice time management you take your life somewhat in your own hands. To be conscious of time is life consciousness.

You Gain Extra Productive Hours

Because of better time management, you gain extra productive hours. You tend to be more disciplined when at work instead of talking about gossip with your co-workers or aimlessly browsing the internet.

Image if you had 1 extra productive hour in a day. That is 5 extra hours in a working week and around 250 hours in a whole year, that's 6 extra weeks of work in a whole year.

You Have Better Control Over Your Life

When you practice time management, you can control the way your life goes. You have a better perception of what work you can do and what work will be done.

You are better organized and prevent deadlines from becoming a problem. Deadline emergencies are unknown to you, instead you spend your time relaxing when others are stressing about work.

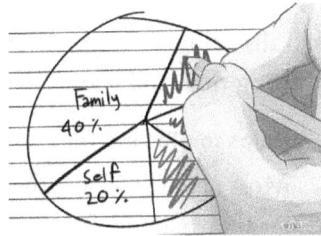

Don't be afraid that you'll become rigid and stiff with your time. It'll actually be the opposite. You'll gain more freedom because you're less dependent of outside events to control your time. Now, you control your time and not someone else.

Life Presents Too Many Distractions

Life today presents so many distractions that it is so easy to lose time on unimportant activities. Ask yourself, is watching this or that TV program, reading this or that gossip or participating in a certain

Everyone is the servant of eternal time, and therefore no one can be king in this material world. King means the person who can order. The celebrated English king wanted to order time and tide, but the time and tide refused to obey his order.

~ Srila Prabhupada (Srimad Bhagavatam 1.13.18)

activity is going to add anything to your life. Is the time spent on a particular activity well spent, or is just a waste of time and energy?

Time management helps you make conscious choices, so you can spend more of your time doing things that are important and valuable to you.

Life Comes Up With So Many Choices

Life puts in front of everyone so many choices each day, and the question is, do you follow what appears on your way, or do you consciously choose what you want to do? Do you allow external distractions deter you from your goal, or do you use willpower and self discipline to walk toward your goal in a straight line, without wasting time and energy?

Helps You To Find Time

Most people feel like they have too much to do and not enough time. They blame lack of time for their poor finances, unachieved goals, stress, bad relationships, lack of spirituality and not exercising their body. Wise time management can help you find the time for what you desire to do or need to do.

Inspires You To Do Things You Do Not Like

Why is time management important? Simple, when you write down what you need to do – it is there staring at you. You are forced to tackle it. To me it is a target I have given myself and so I must live up to the challenge regardless of how much I hate doing it.

Limited, Precious Resource

When you plan your time you are making wise investment of a very limited and precious resource – time. Knowing what to work on, when and how much time you have to finish the work makes you more focused.

Getting Started With Time Management

Creates a Positive Cycle

There is a multiplicative benefit involved here. Implementing time management allows you to accomplish more in less time. This saves time which in turn lowers your stress levels. This in turn increases your attention span and increases your work quality, which leads to better accomplishment and effectiveness. Each benefit of time management impacts other aspects of your life and it becomes a cycle where things keep getting better every time.

Reference:

Long Yun Siang, Career Success For Newbies

Horton, Thomas. New York The CEO Paradox (1992)

"Tyranny of the Urgent" essay by Charles Hummel 1967

Time

A Daily Miracle

The supply of time is a daily miracle. You wake up in the morning and lo! Your purse is magnificently filled with 24 hours of the unmanufactured tissue of the universe of life. It is yours! The most precious of your possessions. No one can take it from you. And no one receives either more or less than you receive.

Philosophers have explained space. They have not explained time fully. It is the inexplicable raw material of everything. With it, all is possible; without it, nothing. The supply of time is truly a daily miracle, an affair genuinely astonishing when one examines it. You wake up in the morning, and lo! your purse is magically filled with twenty-four hours of the unmanufactured tissue of the universe of your life! It is yours. It is the most precious of possessions. A highly singular commodity, showered upon you in a manner as singular as the commodity itself!

For remark! No one can take it from you. It is unstealable. And no one receives either more or less than you receive.

Talk about an ideal democracy! In the realm of time there is no aristocracy of wealth, and no aristocracy of intellect. Genius is never

"Nothing really belongs to us but time, which even he has who has nothing else." ~ Bennett, Arnold

rewarded by even an extra hour a day. And there is no punishment. Waste your infinitely precious commodity as much as you will, and the supply will never be withheld from you. No mysterious power will say:—"This man is a fool, if not a knave. He does not deserve time; he shall be cut off at the meter." It is more certain than consols, and payment of income is not affected by Sundays. Moreover, you cannot draw on the future. Impossible to get into debt! You can only waste the passing moment. You cannot waste to-morrow; it is kept for you. You cannot waste the next hour; it is kept for you.

We said the affair was a miracle. Is it not?

You have to live on this twenty-four hours of daily time. Out of it you have to spin health, pleasure, money, content, respect, and the evolution of your immortal soul. Its right use, its most effective use, is a matter of the highest urgency and of the most thrilling actuality. All depends on that. Your happiness — the elusive prize that you are all clutching for, my friends! — depends on that.

Strange that the newspapers, so enterprising and up-to-date as they are, are not full of "How to live on a given income of time," instead of "How to live on a given income of money"! Money is far commoner than time. When one reflects, one perceives that money

> "A man may desire to go to Mecca. He may perish ingloriously on the coast of the Red Sea... but he will not be tormented in the same way as the man who, desiring to reach Mecca, never leaves Brixton. Most of us have not left Brixton. We have not even taken a cab to Ludgate Circus and inquired from Cook's the price of a conducted tour. And our excuse to ourselves is that there are only twenty-four hours in the day."
> ~ Arnold Bennett

is just about the commonest thing there is. It encumbers the earth in gross heaps.

If one can't contrive to live on a certain income of money, one earns a little more — or steals it, or begs or borrows it. One doesn't necessarily muddle one's life because one can't quite manage on a small monthly income. But if one cannot arrange that a 'time income' of twenty-four hours a day shall exactly cover all proper items of time expenditure, one does muddle one's life definitely. The supply of time, though gloriously regular, is cruelly restricted.

We never shall have any more time. We have, and we have always had, all the time there is. It is the realisation of this profound and neglected truth that should lead us to the minute practical examination of daily time-expenditure.

Reference:

How to Live on 24 Hours a Day, Arnold Bennett, 1910

This sun's business is to take away the portion, the fixed up duration of life which I have been given. That is, some of it, is taken away. The same example. Just like you have got a fixed balance in the bank. If you draw even ten pence, ten shillings, that means it is taken away. You have to replace it. But in case of life's duration, replacing is not possible. Bank balance you can replace. But this balance you can not. Suppose if I will live for eighty years or ninety years or hundred years. So this seventy-eight years (my present age) is already taken away. It cannot be replaced.
  ~ Srila Prabhupada (Srimad-Bhāgavatam 1.16.6 -- Los Angeles, January 3, 1974)

Seize The Day

Yesterday Is Dead And Gone

And Tomorrow Is Out Of Sight

Now Until Bed Time Is All You Have

Christ's prayer, "Give us this day our daily bread", asks only for today's bread. It doesn't complain about the stale bread we had to eat yesterday; and it doesn't say: "Oh, God, it has been pretty dry out in the wheat belt lately and we may have another drought-and then how will I get bread to eat next autumn-or suppose I lose my job-oh, God, how could I get bread then?"

No, this prayer teaches us to ask for today's bread only. Today's bread is the only kind of bread you can possibly eat.

Jesus says, "Take therefore no thought for the morrow; for the morrow shall take thought for the things of itself. Sufficient unto the day is the evil thereof."

We are standing this very second at the meeting-place of two eternities: the vast past that has endured for ever, and the future that is plunging on to the last syllable of recorded time. We can't possibly live in either of those eternities-no, not even for one split second. But, by trying to do so, we can wreck both our bodies and our minds. *So let's be content to live the only time we can possibly live: from now until bedtime.*

"Anyone can carry his burden, however hard, until nightfall," wrote Robert Louis Stevenson. "Anyone can do his work, however hard, for one day. Anyone can live sweetly, patiently, lovingly, purely, till the sun goes down. And this is all that life really means."

Five hundred years before Christ was born, the Greek philosopher Heraclitus told his students that "everything changes except the law of change". He said: "You cannot step in the same river twice." The river changes every second; and so does the man who stepped in it. Life is a ceaseless change. The only certainty is today. Why mar the beauty of living today by trying to solve the problems of a future that is shrouded in ceaseless change and uncertainty - a future that no one can possibly foretell?

The old Romans had a word for it. In fact, they had two words for it. Carpe diem. "Enjoy the day. " Or, "Seize the day." Yes, seize the day, and make the most of it.

That is the philosophy of Lowell Thomas. He had these words from Psalm CXVIII framed and hanging on the walls of his broadcasting studio where he would see them often:

"This is the day which the Lord hath made; we will rejoice and be glad in it."

John Ruskin had on his desk a simple piece of stone on which was carved one word: TODAY.

Famous Indian dramatist, Kalidasa wrote a poem:

Salutation To The Dawn
Look to this day!
For it is life, the very life of life.
In its brief course
Lie all the verities and realities of your existence:
The bliss of growth
The glory of action
The splendour of achievement.
For yesterday is but a dream

And tomorrow is only a vision,
But today well lived makes yesterday a dream of happiness
And every tomorrow a vision of hope.
Look well, therefore, to this day!
Such is the salutation to the dawn.

Reference:

How To Stop Worrying And Start Living, Dale Carnegie, 1948

Forster, Mark (2006-07-20). Do It Tomorrow and Other Secrets of Time Management. Hodder & Stoughton Religious. p. 224. ISBN 0-340-90912-9.

So we should be very, very careful that this human form of life should not be wasted even for a moment. That is real life. There is, by, one sloka by Rūpa Gosvāmi. Avyartha-kālatvam [Cc.Madhya 23.18-19]. A devotee should always be alert to see, "Whether this time, one moment passed, whether I have wasted it or I have utilized it?" That is, should be, the point.
~ Srila Prabhupada (Srimad-Bhagavatam 5.5.16 -- Vrndāvana, November 4, 1976)

To Catch Some Dreams

You Need Running Shoes

Luck Is Fascinated With The Efficient

S uccess is a vehicle, which moves on a wheel named hard work. There is no taking it easy. It would be difficult to name any one who has gotten to the top without hard work. Hard work might not always get you to the top, but it will get you pretty near.

David Bly says, "Striving for success without hard work is like looking for fruit in places that you didn't plant seeds! It's completely useless." According to Confucius, "Man who stand on hill with mouth open will wait long time for roast duck to drop in. "

To think too long about doing a thing often becomes its undoing. One worthwhile task carried to a successful conclusion is worth half-a-hundred half-finished tasks.

In Hitopadesh, the great Sanskrit text it is said,
'Udyamen hi sidhyanti, karyaani na manorathaih
Nahi suptasya singhasya, pravishanti mukhe mrigah'
Translated, it means;
Action and not the will alone, makes the wishes come true
The deer would not walk into the mouth of a lion asleep

This is further explained in the following fables.

Don't count Your Chicken Before They Hatch

A Milk-maid had been to the meadow to milk her cows. Now she was returning home with a pail of milk on her head.

She thought, "I will make cream and butter out of this milk. Then selling them, I will buy eggs. and when they hatch, I shall have a good poultry farm."

She further thought, "I shall sell some of my fowls and buy a fine dress. Seeing it on my body at the fair, all the boys will admire me. But I will turn them away just tossing my head at them."

Lost in day dreams, she forgot about the pail on her head. She tossed her head with a jerk and the pail of milk came tumbling down. It was broken and all the milk got spilt.

God Helps Those Who Help Themselves

There was a flood in a village. One man said to everyone as they evacuated, "I'll stay! God will save me! In God I trust and in this hour of crisis, I will not betray Him."

The flood waters got higher and a boat came along. The driver yelled "Come on mate, get in!" "No" replied the man. "God will save me!"

So long we have got this body we have to do something. Without doing something we cannot live. The material world will not allow you, that you cannot do anything and you'll be provided. No. Whatever you may be, you may be President Nixon or ordinary man in the street, everyone has to do something. That is not possible. There is a verse in the Visnu Purana, trtiya-saktir isyate [Cc. Madhya 6.154]. There the situation, material situation, is so stringent, that without working, you cannot live. You'll die.

~ Srila Prabhupada (Lecture, Bhagavad-gita 2.40 - London, September 13, 1973)

The flood waters further rose and the man had to stand on the roof of his house. A helicopter soon arrived and a rope ladder was lowered. "No, God will save me!" he said.

Eventually the man drown. He got by the gates of heaven and said to God, "Why didn't you save me? I had full trust in you."

God replied, "For goodness sake! I sent a boat and a helicopter. What more do you want!"

Focused Action

Beats Brilliance

O ne of the major causes of personal failure is the lack of persistence in carrying through that which one begins. Imagine a person planting his shrub every week in a new place. It will never have time to get a footing. Or a person digging a well and abandoning it after a while and going to another spot to dig again. To get the water, the digging has to be persistently carried out.

Therefore 'one worthwhile task carried to a successful conclusion is worth half-a-hundred half-finished tasks.'

If you take the time to study any successful person, you will learn that the vast majority of them have had more 'failures' than they have had 'successes'. This is because successful people are persistent; the more they stumble and fall, the more they get right back up and get going again.

On the other hand, people that don't get back up and try again, never reach success. Srila Prabhupada, founder of Hare Krishna Movement, finally succeeded in his efforts at the ripe age of 70. And this too after facing many failures. Walt Disney was turned down 302 times before he got financing for his dream of creating the "happiest place on Earth".

Calvin Coolidge rightly puts it, "Nothing in the world will take the place of persistence. Talent will not; nothing is more common than the unsuccessful person with talent. Genius will not; unrewarded genius is almost a proverb. Education will not; the world is full of educated derelicts. Persistence and determination alone are omnipotent."

And according to Hubbard, "Many people fail in life, not for lack of ability or brains or even courage but simply because they have never organized their energies around a goal."

It is wonderful how much can be done if we are always doing.

Everyone knows the story concerning a hare who ridicules a slow-moving tortoise and is challenged by the tortoise to a race. The hare soon leaves the tortoise behind and, confident of winning, takes a nap midway

"My dad says persistence is the key to success. So I'm going to keep giving you the same wrong answer until it becomes the right answer!"

through the course. When the Hare awakes however, he finds that his competitor, crawling slowly but steadily, has arrived before him.

Therefore Bible advises, 'the race is not to the swift' (Ecclesiastes 9.11). And according to Croxall, 'the more haste, the worse speed'.

In classical times it was not the tortoise's plucky conduct in taking on a bully that was emphasised but the hare's foolish over-confidence. An old Greek source comments that 'many people have good natural abilities which are ruined by idleness; on the other hand, sobriety, zeal and perseverance can prevail over indolence.

When a baby learns to walk and talk – they don't get anything right at first. Can you imagine condemning them to a life of crawling because they don't rise and walk on their first effort? Or, relegating them to a life of silence because they don't utter their first sentence perfectly? Crazy, isn't it?

But the baby has cheerleaders constantly encouraging them, loving them, and teaching them. And they persist – and nearly every one of them learns to walk and talk. Imagine that!

Perhaps we are at a point that we don't have those daily cheerleaders so readily any more. It's easier to quit when there's no one watching or encouraging us constantly to keep going. It's at these very moments that your cheerleading is simply your persistence.

Therefore Arnold Bennett advises, "Let the pace of the first lap be even absurdly slow, but let it be as regular as possible."

And Don't try to bite off more than you can chew: If you want to start doing something new, give yourself space to do it slowly, comfortably. The most important thing is that you do it consistently:

Determination means continuing to practice .....with patience and perseverance. If one does not immediately attain the desired results, one should not think, "Oh, what is this ...? I will give it up." No, we must have determination and faith.

In this regard, there is a mundane example. When a young girl gets married, she immediately hankers for a child. She thinks, "Now I am married. I must have a child immediately." But how is this possible? The girl must have patience, become a faithful wife, serve her husband, and let her love grow. Eventually, because she is married, it is certain that she will have a child. Similarly, when we are in Krsna consciousness, our perfection is guaranteed, but we must have patience and determination. We should think, "I must execute my duties and should not be impatient." Impatience is due to loss of determination.
~ Srila Prabhupada (Path of Perfection 5: Determination and Steadiness in Yoga)

Be Wise

Early Rise

Win The Battle of The Bed

There will be plenty of time to sleep when you are dead. Loose an hour in the morning and you will be looking for it the rest of the day.

Waking up early is a productivity method of rising early and consistently so as to be able to accomplish more during the day. Morning time is the best time because the highways of brain are not clogged by the traffic of distracting thoughts.

Imagine driving down to some place early in the morning and driving down again to the same place in the peak hour. What you could comfortably traverse in ten minutes might take two hours during the peak hour. Similar is the case with our brain. As the day progresses, the neuronic highways of brain become clogged by the clutter of daily life and the speed of data passing through them slows down considerably.

> *The time early in the morning, one and a half hours before sunrise, is called brahma-muhūrta. During this brahma-muhūrta, spiritual activities are recommended. Spiritual activities performed early in the morning have a greater effect than in any other part of the day.*
> ~ Srila Prabhupada (SB 3.20.46)

Therefore early morning is the best period to do things that are important in your life. Vedic literatures recommend getting up 1 hour 48 minutes before the Sunrise. This is known as 'Brahma Muhurta". This is the time when chakras or energy centers in our bodies are perfectly aligned and our cognitive faculties are at their best.

Early rising has been recommended since antiquity and is presently recommended by all personal development gurus. The philosopher Aristotle said, "It is well to be up before daybreak, for such habits contribute to health, wealth, and wisdom."

A habit of waking up early can be developed through practice and preparation. Within the context of religious observances, spiritual writers have called this practice "the heroic minute", referring to the sacrifice which this entails.

Early to bed and early to rise makes a man Healthy, wealthy, and wise.
Benjamin Franklin

Benjamin Franklin is quoted to have said: "Early to bed and early to rise, makes a man healthy, wealthy and wise". It is a saying

At night we are wasting time. The so long we sleep, that is wasting time. The less we sleep... And even a very, very big businessmen, they sleep very less. Very, very big politician, they also sleep less. So because sleeping, the part of our life spended sleeping that means wasted. So we should control our sleeping, not to sleep more. That is one of the business. Because our life is very short, and if we spend our time sleeping... Suppose half sleeping and half working. Then half our life is spoiled simply by sleeping. Then other business are there. In old age we cannot do anything. In childhood we cannot do anything substantial. So childhood means up to twenty years we spoil. And then, when we get old, we spend another twenty years—forty years. And suppose we live eighty years. So eighty years, out of eighty years, another twenty years by sleeping, then we get twenty years. (laughter) But our business is very responsible, that we have to solve all the problems of life.

~ Srila Prabhupada (Srimad-Bhāgavatam 6.1.15 -- Auckland, February 22, 1973)

that is viewed as a commonsensical proverb. He is also quoted as saying: "The early morning has gold in its mouth", a translation of the German proverb "Morgenstund hat Gold im Mund".

"The early bird gets the worm" is a proverb that suggests that getting up early will lead to success during the day.

According to Victor Hugo, there is no time like early morning to do your time management, "He who every morning plans the transaction of the day and follows out the plan, carries a thread that will guide him through the labyrinth of the most busy life."

Live As If

You'll Die Tomorrow

And One Day You Will Be Right

Death, the ultimate deadline, allows us to cherish both life and time more fully.

There is no reason why we cannot consciously apply the urgency that death brings to our everyday lives. Indeed, we should. Steve Jobs was fond of saying, "Live everyday as though it is your last … and one day, you will be right."

All the flowers of all of the tomorrows are in the seeds of today. If we maintain this awareness that today could be our last, we would be inspired to utilize this day in a much wiser way. It is said:

Each day it opens a new account for us.

Each night it burns the remains of the day.

If we fail to use the day's deposits, the loss is ours.

If we take care of today God will take care of tomorrow.

And a Sanskrit poet says:

For yesterday is but a memory

and tomorrow is only a vision;

but today well lived

makes every yesterday a memory of happiness

and every tomorrow a vision of hope.

Look well, therefore, to this day!"

Mary Jean Irion prays, "Normal day, let me be aware of the treasure you are. Let me learn from you, love you, savor you, bless you before you depart. Let me not pass you by in quest of some rare and perfect tomorrow. Let me hold you while I may, for it will not always be so. One day I shall...bury my face in the pillow, or raise my hands to the sky, and want, more than all the world your return."

George Eliot laments, "The golden moments in the stream of life rush past us and we see nothing but sand; the angels come to visit us, and we only know them when they are gone."

William Blake advises to see, if we can, eternity in the hour that passes.

To see the world in a grain of sand,
and to see heaven in a wild flower,
hold infinity in the palm of your hands,
and eternity in an hour.

An unknown author has similar advice:
This is the beginning of a new day.
God has given me this day to use as I will.
I can waste it or use it for good.
What I do today is important, because
I am exchanging a day of my life for it.
When tomorrow comes,
this day will be gone forever,
leaving in its place something
that I have traded for it.
I want it to be gain, not loss;
good not evil; success not failure;
in order that I shall not regret
the price I paid for it.

What If I Told You That You Were Going To Die Tomorrow?

Please raise your hand if you are not going to die.

If you haven't found the fountain of youth and we haven't perfected anti-aging technology, then you my friend are going to die. But you are not alone, so am I, and so is your mother and your father and your brothers and sisters.

Now that I have reminded you of your own mortality. Does this change anything in your life?

Probably not.

What if I told you that you were going to die tomorrow? Does this change anything in your life?

Probably so.

Why is this? Why does a timeline, or a "deadline" make a difference for us?

I believe that a deadline changes the quality of the preceding moments. Some moments in life merely pass, forgetably, almost as if unattended, but other moments are imbued with great meaning and even urgency, particularly if we know that those moments are to be our last, as with a departing friend or dying lover. These last moments are often the ones in which we feel most alive and most present.

DEATH WORKS FROM HOME

Should we rob anyone of these meaningful moments?

No. The mere thought seems cruel and deeply inhumane.

Yet, if we do not speak of death and its reality, and especially its proximity, then we have robbed ourselves and our loved ones of the power of last moments.

When a doctor does not speak the truth and does not say the words, "Yes, you are dying," then you are robbed of the opportunity to live fully in the present, savoring or utilizing what is left of your life.

What human would rob another of the most touching and beautiful moments of life?

We do this all of the time, to ourselves and those whom we love, if we don't speak the truth about death and its timing. In private, we ask the doctor "not to tell her how sick she really is." Yet, the words, "You probably only have another month left," could prove to be among the best therapies that your doctor could ever give you.

Because of those words, each day, each hour, each second of that month would be seen in a different light than any time that had ever passed before. Each moment cherished, devoured hungrily, and deeply savored. Precious time, never squandered, but focused only on those things which matter most.

And you will love this quote by John A. Robinson: "Make the most out of each day you have. Do not live to die, die to live each day to its fullest. Say what you need to say and do what you need

---

Pariksit Maharaja was given a warning notice that he would meet death within seven days, and he at once left his palace to prepare himself for the next stage. The king had at least seven days at his disposal in which to prepare for death, but as far as we are concerned, although at least we know that our death is sure, we have no information of the date fixed for the occurrence. I do not know whether I am going to meet death at the next moment. Even such a great man as Mahatma Gandhi could not calculate that he was going to meet with death in the next five minutes, nor could his great associates guess his impending death. Nonetheless, all such gentlemen present themselves as great leaders of the people.

It is ignorance of death and life that distinguishes an animal from a man. A man, in the real sense of the term, inquires about himself and what he is. Wherefrom has he come into this life, and where is he going after death? Why is he put under the troubles of threefold miseries although he does not want them? Beginning from one's childhood, one goes on inquiring about so many things in his life, but he never inquires about the real essence of life. This is animalism. There is no difference between a man and an animal as far as the four principles of animal life are concerned, for every living being exists by eating, sleeping, fearing, and mating. But only the human life is meant for relevant inquiries into the facts about eternal life and the Transcendence. Human life is therefore meant for research into eternal life, and the Vedanta-sutra advises one to conduct this research now or never.
~ Srila Prabhupada (Science of Self Rrealization : The Art of Dying)

---

to do, because at any time, that chance can become history without warning."

From tomorrow, let us be more focused on the use and cultivation of our time and our life. Let us savor it, every drop.

Reference:

Monica Williams-Murphy, Md, January 10, 2013

When Yudhisthira Maharaja was asked, "What is the most wonderful thing in the world?" he replied, "The most wonderful thing is that every day, every moment, people are dying, and yet everyone thinks that death will not come for him." Every minute and every second we experience that living entities are going to the temple of death. Men, insects, animals, birds -- everyone is going. This world, therefore, is called mrtyuloka -- the planet of death. Every day there are obituaries, and if we bother to go to the cemetery or crematorium grounds we can validate them. Yet everyone is thinking, "Somehow or other I'll live." Everyone is subject to the law of death, yet no one takes it seriously. This is illusion. Thinking we will live forever, we go on doing whatever we like, feeling that we will never be held responsible. This is a very risky life, and it is the densest part of illusion. We should become very serious and understand that death is waiting. We have heard the expression, "as sure as death." This means that in this world death is the most certain thing; no one can avoid it. When death comes, no longer will our puffed-up philosophy or advanced degrees help us. At that time our stout and strong body and our intelligence -- which don't care for anything -- are vanquished. At that time the fragmental portion (jivatma) comes under the dictation of material nature, and prakrti (nature) gives us the type of body for which we are fit. If we want to take this risk, we can avoid Krsna;
~ Srila Prabhupada (Raja Vidya 2: Knowledge Beyond Samsara)

Life Is Uncertain

And Death Is Sure

Uncertainty Is The Only Certainty There Is

Uncertainty is the only certainty there is, and knowing how to live with insecurity is the only security. Therefore Benjamin Franklin advises, "Since thou are not sure of a minute, throw not away an hour." There is no guarantee that we will live through the next minute. Anytime anything can transpire.

The Wisdom of Uncertainty

There is an old story about a Russian farmer in the late 1800's, who happened to own a horse. As you can imagine, back then if you had a horse you were considered a person of property. A horse could help you work the land, you could rent it out to your neighbors, it was reliable transportation, and so forth. This farmer, therefore, was considered very fortunate.

"How lucky you are to have a horse!" his neighbors would tell him.

"You never know," the farmer would always reply.

One night, a sudden and violent storm blew up, and the frightened horse broke down the fence of the corral and got away.

"How unlucky you are to have lost your horse!" they all said.

"You never know," replied the farmer.

Sure enough, a few days later his horse returned, accompanied by a beautiful wild stallion.

"Two horses! How lucky you are!" everyone told the farmer, who only said, "You never know."

The farmer had a son, which was another good thing to have in those days. Extra hands were always needed to do the chores around the place, and this particular young man was strong and hard-working, so he decided to tame the wild stallion.

"He looks so natural."

While doing so, however, he was thrown from the horse and broke his leg.

"Your son broke his leg!" the neighbors lamented. "How terrible!"

"You never know," said the farmer.

A great Indian scientist, busy in the planmaking business, was suddenly called by invincible eternal time while going to attend a very important meeting of the planning commission, and he had to surrender his life, wife, children, house, land, wealth, etc. During the political upsurge in India and its division into Pakistan and Hindustan, so many rich and influential Indians had to surrender life, property and honor due to the influence of time, and there are hundreds and thousands of examples like that all over the world, all over the universe, which are all effects of the influence of time. Therefore, the conclusion is that there is no powerful living being within the universe who can overcome the influence of time. Many poets have written verses lamenting the influence of time. Many devastations have taken place over the universes due to the influence of time, and no one could check them by any means. Even in our daily life, so many things come and go in which we have no hand, but we have to suffer or tolerate them without remedial measure. That is the result of time.

~ Srila Prabhupada (Srimad Bhagavatam 1.13.20)

Less than a week later, Cossacks swept through the village and neighboring farms, and conscripted every able-bodied young man for service in the army. Since the farmer's son was unable to walk or ride with his broken leg, he was not taken.

And so it goes...

The fact is that we never know what is going to happen next, and we never know what fortune, good or ill, will arise out of any event. Alan Watts coined the phrase "the wisdom of uncertainty" to describe the existential fact that the seeds for our enlightenment rest in the unexpected events of our lives, not in our constant and fruitless search for security.

Life at times can be very uncertain. Our uncertainty can either cripple us or cause us to further live by faith.

Without uncertainty and the unknown, life becomes the stale repetition of outworn memories. You become a victim of the past, and your tormentor today is your self left over from yesterday.

Today, factor the unexpected into your plans. Experiment with letting life take you where it wants to go, and begin to trust that this path will lead to something new and exciting. By releasing the tight fist of clinging to an imagined outcome, you will find freedom.

Reference:
Roger Nolan

Deadlines

And Their Productive Power

The Best Way To Predict The Future Is To Create It.

If it weren't for the last minute, nothing would ever get done. It is often seen that deadline makes us perform faster. Work follows Parkinson's law, "Work expands so as to fill the time available for its completion." It is seen in case of journalists that they write better when stimulated by a deadline. We all have a love/hate relationship with them, but we also know that without them nothing would have been completed.

According to Steve Smith, "A goal is a dream with a deadline," John Shanahan says, "Deadlines are the mothers of invention".

Use The Power Of Deadlines

Put your requests into a time frame. If there is no pressing time frame, make one up.

If you want a report from someone, finish your request by asking, "And may I have this by the end of our business day Thursday?"

Various dictionaries describe a deadline as a time by which something must be done; originally meaning "a line that does not move," and "a line around a military prison beyond which an escaping prisoner could be shot."

Literally, it is line over which the person or project becomes dead! Deadlines propel action. So when you want to get people into action, give them a deadline.

If you make a request without including a date or time, then you don't have anything that you can hold the other person accountable for. You have a "wished for" and "hoped for" action hanging out there in space with no time involved. People are only motivated when we use both space and time. The space-time continuum is a motivator's best friend.

Once, an author was leisurely writing a book when the publisher called back to impose a month-away deadline to make the catalog for the big Christmas sales season. Then, all of a sudden, he swung into gear, writing and editing 20 hours a day, until he delivered the finished manuscript to the publisher. It turned out to be the best-written book he'd ever done.

Without a deadline, there is no goal, just a nebulous request that adds to the general confusion at work. You will be doing a person a favor by putting your request into a time frame. And if the time is too short, he or she can negotiate it. Let your people participate. It isn't a matter of who gets to set the deadline, it's a matter of having one. Either way, it is settled, clear, and complete.

Most managers don't do this. They have hundreds of unfulfilled requests floating around the workplace, because they aren't prioritized. Those requests keep getting put off.

Don't they? Deadlines will fix all that.

The Productivity Power of Deadlines

by Andrea Dekker

I have many, many deadlines, both in my business and personal life -- I'm sure you can relate.

Deadlines to finish a project
Deadlines to ship a big order
Deadlines to send invoices
Deadlines to pay quarterly taxes

Deadlines to RSVP for meetings and other specific events
Deadlines to schedule doctor and dentist appointments
Deadlines to make hotel and/or flight reservations
Deadlines for car repairs and oil changes
My lists could go on and on...

We have deadlines for a reason -- and without them, we'd probably be very late and very unprepared most of the time. There's also a pretty good chance that without deadlines, we'd be much less productive.

So while the deadlines I listed above are somewhat mandatory there are many other deadlines I set for myself that aren't mandatory -- simply because I know I get more done in less time if I use the power of deadlines!

For example, if you have a few long-term projects that don't necessarily need to be finished by any certain time, I can almost guarantee you won't work on them unless you have vast amounts of free time

THE GRAVEYARD of PAST DEADLINES

(which probably won't happen any time soon). So those long-term projects will sit there and sit there while you're busy meeting all your other deadlines.

However, if you give yourself a deadline to complete all, or at least a specific portion, of that long-term project, there's a good chance you'll finish the project way ahead of schedule while still meeting your other deadlines.

Here are a few self-imposed deadlines you might consider:
a deadline to organize your office space
a deadline to clean out your email inbox
a deadline to file that huge pile of papers on your desk
a deadline to set your new business goals

a deadline to unplug and recharge

Obviously, there are 101 things you could add to this list... the point is that by creating deadlines, you're more likely to follow through with whatever it is you want to do.

Even though I'm personally not a procrastinator, I can confidently say that deadlines still give me that extra incentive to "do it now" instead of waiting until later — which ultimately means I get more done in less time!

Parkinson's law - Give Yourself a Little Less Time

Have you ever noticed how tasks expand to fit their deadline? Whether simple task or complex project, they always seem to finish right before their deadline.

They take, well, just as much time as you give them.

Expanding Time = Expanding Projects

Here is a trick question: "How long will that new 6-month project take to finish?"

Answer: At least 6 months.

Why? Because projects fill the time they are allotted.

The interesting question is, "How long would the same project have taken if it was only given 3 months?"

Could the same work have been completed?

Often, especially in corporate environments, the answer is YES.

"Projects and tasks will expand to fit the allowed time even if the full time is not needed."

So, why do we let deadlines be so slack?

Maybe it is because we have come to take deadlines for granted. We expect people not to abide by them, so we give outrageously long time frames in the hope that the work will be completed.

Unfortunately, this often backfires. When the deadline is not met and an extension is granted, an unnecessarily long time has already elapsed.

And of course, that deadline extension leads to another.

The next time you are setting a deadline, set it for less time than you think the task will take.

By keeping tight deadlines, you will increase your productivity and get more done.

Don't underestimate the power of tight deadlines...

Advantages of Deadlines

Ignites Creativity

Nothing can spur creativity and imagination like a tight deadline. If you had one month to do that project instead of six, how would you do it? Sometimes the best ideas come from a lack of time.

Reduces Wasted Time

It is better to err of the side of too little time. When you keep deadlines tight, you avoid unnecessary slack time in your work and projects. If you underestimate the time needed, you can give yourself more time. On the other hand, if you give excessive time, it will be used up by the work.

Encourages Teamwork

Nothing builds relationships like teamwork on a tight deadline. People bond when they work together to meet a common goal or deadline.

Builds Confidence

You stretch your limits when you accomplish something you did not think you could do. Finishing something in less time than you thought possible builds confidence to do even better next time. Often, you are stronger than you think.

Finishes Early

Finishing in less time, allows for review (and even re-work). It also reduces stress. If that report is due in 1 month and you finish it in 3 weeks, you will have extra time to reflect and even improve.

Makes the Impossible Possible

Sometimes it takes a tight deadline to make the impossible happen. When you combine the above powers, you might be amazed at what can be accomplished in a short time frame. Deadline pressure can make magical things happen.

The word's 'crazy', 'freaky', 'tight' and 'terrible' are often used as synonyms of the word 'deadline'.

The next time you are setting the deadline for your work or projects, keep it tight. Give yourself a little less time than you think may be needed. You might surprise yourself. (Or your boss…)

You just might make "Mission Impossible" into "Mission Accomplished."

Trademark Of All High-Performing People

Understanding the power of deadlines and communicating urgency to yourself is a trademark of all high-performing people. High-performing people are the ones who accomplish a lot in life. And they do so by

So how does meeting a dead lion help me learn time management?

delegating their projects to a large team. And a large team without looming deadlines is completely useless.

Antidote of Procrastination

Deadlines make procrastination less likely. If you don't deliver as expected, someone will eventually come around and ask about it. So your first motivator is fear of losing face to those who were counting on you, or a more general fear of letting someone down.

Next, if you don't do something, the someone who was expecting it might inform others. So the second motivator is a fear of losing face among a larger group. Now, not only have you shown your laziness or inability to one person, but several, opening you up to derision or scorn from a larger number of people.

After that, someone with some authority over you will notice – like a boss, higher level client. So the third motivator is the fear of losing the regard of people who are particularly important to you in some way.

At the next level of deadline-missing repercussions, we have the possibility of some kind of retribution, like a confrontation, or a "performance improvement plan". So the fourth motivator is fear of large or small future actions that could harm you in some way.

From there, there is a cascade of fears. Fear of losing your job, your home; depending on the type of deadline you've missed, possibly even your health or your life (dental cleanings and payments on your insurance being obvious examples). Add to this the possible fears of these actions affecting your spouse or business partners, children or employees. Let's take another look at this progression:

Missed a deadline

Fear of losing face to strangers

Fear of losing face to a larger group of strangers

Fear of losing face to someone important to you

Fear of retribution for missed deadline(s)

Fear of loss of job

Fear of loss of income

Fear of loss of health

Fear of loss of life

Deadlines trigger the first step in the chain. They are the first hint that you are on a slippery slope.

Deadlines are the voice that calls us back from the edge, before we step onto the slippery slope. They are one of the most important "canary in the mines" of our life.

How To Self-Motivate Without Deadlines

So what about work with no deadlines? The work that simply needs to be done "sometime"? What if that work is personal, and no one will ever come looking for it? Something like learning a language, or cleaning out your closet, or creating a smarter process for your own work. These are the longer-term goals, the ones that make a real difference to your life/work/achievement. No one will ever follow up to make sure you accomplished those tasks. (Assuming you don't have a teacher, parent, boss or spouse looking over your shoulder.) Your motivation for deadline-free, long-term goals is fear, but possibility. And possibility is not the stuff of instant gratification, like meeting a deadline is.

Here are some tried-and-true advice for how to self-motivate without deadlines:

Write down your goals. While there have been few studies that really looked at the success factor of written goals, most people agree that the act of writing your goals – and reviewing them regularly – helps in achieving them.

Take time to think about what the end game will look like for each of your goals. Imagine it as specifically as you can. For example, if you want to write a case study, imagine what it will look like, whether it will be printed or PDF, who you will share it with, how you will gather feedback. The more specific your mental image, the more likely you are to stay on track.

Ask yourself, "What step can I take right now to make progress on this goal?" We all know that the journey of a thousand miles starts with a single step. And every goal is just a series of small steps toward achievement. If you want to be a great golfer, every ball you hit is another step toward mastery. Let's assume that there are 75 tiny steps on the path to your goal. Tackle one per day and your goal will be complete less than three months from now.

Take that first small step before the end of the day. You'll feel better with some progress under your feet. Use your innate human response to "sunk cost" and "loss aversion" to your advantage. Like a gambler trying to win back losses, you will keep moving forward to avoid having wasted your time. (This effect – for gamblers and procrastinators – gets stronger as you invest more.)

Deadline Pressure: Use It To Your Advantage In Negotiations

Adapted from an article by Don A. Moore published in the Negotiation newsletter.

In the summer of 1988, National Basketball Association (NBA) team owners and players were at loggerheads over their new contract. At midnight on June 30, the owners declared a lockout, halting preparations for the start of the 1998–99 NBA season. The players and owners negotiated for six long months, during which time the two sides collectively lost hundreds of millions of dollars.

In the end, it was a deadline that resolved the conflict. The team owners declared that if they didn't reach an agreement with the players by January 7, 1999, they would cancel the rest of the

Human birth is rare and one's life span brief. Why is human life so precious? Because we can use it for self-realization and get free of birth and death. But, as implied by this sutra, much of our human lifetime is consumed in the struggle for existence.

Whenever we misspend time, it is an irretrievable loss. As Canakya Pandita states, all the gold in a rich man's possession cannot buy back a single moment of time.

~ Srila Prabhupada (Narada Bhakti Sutra 77)

season. In effect, the owners placed a final, arbitrary deadline on their participation in the negotiations; the chosen date had little significance to either side. Through public statements, the owners committed themselves to declaring an impasse if the deadline came and went. In the early-morning hours of January 6, the two sides agreed to contract terms that dramatically favored the owners.

We're all familiar with stories of tough opponents who bargain for months without making progress, only to reach resolution in the final moments before the passage of a critical deadline. Without a deadline, negotiators are tempted to use stalling tactics, hoping to pressure the other side into giving in.

Despite the proven effectiveness of deadlines, they remain one of the most misunderstood negotiation strategies. Many negotiators hesitate to place a deadline on their talks. In his research, when professor Don Moore of Carnegie Mellon University asked people to predict the effect of deadlines on negotiations, even experienced negotiators predicted that the presence of a shared deadline would hurt them by forcing them to concede more quickly than they would like, thereby helping their opponents.

While there is some truth to these assumptions, it's also true that deadlines increase pressure on the other party to reach an agreement. Negotiators who recognize that deadlines affect everyone equally can use them to defuse costly stalling tactics. For example, car salespeople sometimes try to draw out price negotiations, hoping the amount of time you've invested will increase your commitment to making the deal. To defuse this strategy, try beginning your negotiation for a new car by informing the salesperson that you have only an hour to make a possible deal.

Because deadlines put pressure on everyone, they can get talks moving again. Don't be afraid to set deadlines and commit to them. Furthermore, when negotiators tell their opponents about an existing final deadline, they get better deals. Why? First, because both sides are more likely to work toward an agreement before the deadline passes, you reduce your risk of walking away with nothing.

Second, when an opponent knows about your deadline, he'll make concessions much more quickly.

References

Wright, Robert (1995). The moral animal : evolutionary psychology and everyday life (1st Vintage books ed. ed.). New York: Vintage Books.

How To Motivate People

The Productivity Power of Deadlines, Andrea Dekker

Barbara A. Marinak and Linda B. Gambrell, "Intrinsic Motivation and Rewards: What Sustains Young Children's Engagement with Text?, " Literacy Research and Instruction 47, 2008, 9-26.

The power of deadlines, Pon Staff On February 2010 / Crisis Negotiations, Daily

The Power of Tight Deadlines, Craig Jarrow

The Power of Deadlines, Petr Tichy, June 2013

The Self-Motivating Power of Deadlines, November 2013, Amy Roffmann New

There Is No Better Time

Than Now

There is no better time than now: Stop telling yourself you'll do something once you're ready, more qualified, or better equipped. Starting is a skill in itself – and one that no other factors will affect deeply enough to validate your waiting. Just do it.

Arnold Bennett says, "There is no magic method of beginning. If a man standing on the edge of a swimming-bath and wanting to jump into the cold water should ask you, 'How do I begin to jump?' you would merely reply, 'Just jump. Take hold of your nerves and jump…. You may fancy the water will be warmer next week. It won't. It will be colder."

The best way to get something done is to begin. Follow Nike on their slogan, 'Just do it'.

A thousand mile journey begins with the first step.

If we don't start, it's certain we can't arrive.

In the words of St. Francis of Assisi, "Start by doing what's necessary, then what's possible, and suddenly you are doing the impossible."

The hardest part is often just starting. It's especially hard to start when a task is difficult or complex. The more importance and weight a certain activity has in your life or business, the more you seem to put off starting.

However, if you can just get moving on it, even for a few minutes, it tends to get easier.

Forget About Finishing, Resolve To Start

Rather than setting the intention to finish something, resolve yourself to start. The more often you start, the easier things get finished. Overcoming that first bit of inertia is the biggest challenge (just like getting started on a run, or the first push of getting a car moving). In a rocket launch, lift off consumes most of the energy. After lift off, cruising takes very little effort.

Once things are moving, momentum is on your side.

Out of thousands and even millions of ignorant people who are wasting their time simply gratifying their senses, one may come to the platform of knowledge and understand higher values of life. Such a person is called a Jnani.

~ Srila Prabhupada (Nectar of Instruction 10)

Busyness and Violence

Of Modern Life

Modern life is characterized by speed. Everything is fast - traffic, food, technology, media and education. We have forgotten the saying - those who rush arrive first at the grave. There is more to life than increasing its speed.

But there are still parts of the world where people live a slow, leisurely life. For example take the case of Indonesian Borneo. Daily life in Borneo's upcountry is usually pleasantly dull, as chickens scratch around, the women fan rice on mats to dry it, thunderstorms roll through, the sun dries the muddy paths, flowers riot into bloom, and it all starts over again the next day. Pastoral Mongolia partially fits the category, too, with its world revolving around camels and sheep rather than rice and bananas.

Learn to pause...or nothing worthwhile will catch up to you, says Doug King. Thomas Merton made an important observation on busyness and the violence of modern life

"The rush and pressure of modern life are a form, perhaps the most common form, of its innate violence. To allow oneself to be carried away by a multitude of conflicting concerns, to surrender to too many demands, to commit oneself to too many projects, to want to help everyone in everything is to succumb to violence. More than that, it is cooperation in violence. The frenzy of the activist...

destroys his own inner capacity for peace. It destroys the fruitfulness of his own work, because it kills the root of inner wisdom which makes work fruitful."

To think he wrote this half a century ago. What would he say now? What would he think of computers, email, cell phones-- technologies that were intended to make life easier, and can, when kept in balance, but in the end have made "the rush and pressure of modern life" worse than ever.

There are many people today who no longer truly take a vacation, because wherever they go they take their work with them. People are using their phones to check and send messages in all possible situations imaginable.

It is not that the technology is bad. It is the way we let it control us. Merton describes this dominant busyness of life as violence. That might sound startling. And he says that giving in to it is to cooperate in violence.

We have created a society that overly values both work and entertainment, and people use technology to switch off one form of busyness and switch on the other. This is violence. It is violence first of all to the human person, because we cannot either know or become our true selves if we don't have regular periods of reflection free from distraction.

Second, the busyness in both work and entertainment serves primarily material purposes, which are endlessly promoted as fulfilling hopes and dreams. The genius of the system is that, even though these hopes and dreams cannot possibly be fulfilled materialistically, the tendency of the chronically distracted is not to doubt the system, but to become willing cogs in the great machine.

This is another form of violence to the human individual, and also feeds other forms of violence, such as crime, war, and environmental destruction.

Coping With Your Crazy Busy Life

Dr. Edward Hallowell, psychiatrist and founder of The Hallowell Center for Cognitive and Emotional Health, was a faculty member at Harvard Medical School in the 1990s when he began to see an upsurge in the number of people who complained about being chronically inattentive, disorganized and overbooked. Many came to him wondering if they had Attention Deficit Disorder (ADD). While some did, most did not. Instead, they had what he called "a severe case of modern life." This imitator was not true attention deficit disorder, but rather an environmental stand-in.

Now a renowned author, Dr. Hallowell talked with BeWell about how the hectic pace of modern life has led our society to suffer from broader, culturally-induced ADD. Dr. Hallowell explores this phenomenon in his book, CrazyBusy: Overstretched, Overbooked, and About to Snap!

In the following interview, we have taken the liberty of incorporating key excerpts from this examination of our frenzied lives and the ways we can better manage how we really want to live.

Why do we like being "crazy busy"?

On a physiological level, being "crazy busy" makes people feel important. If you are busy, then you must be in demand. This is not necessarily true, of course. And, on a physiological level, you get a rush each time you speed through something. You can get hooked on that feeling and become an adrenaline junkie. Speed is a form

of ecstasy. In short, we get off on it, so we crave it and then start to demand it.

Modern life makes us feel as if we can be everywhere and do everything and it gives us magical tools that heighten the illusion. Watch the modern mother coordinating the schedules of three children, her career, her pet, and herself: how did she ever do it before cell phones, email and voicemail? As harried as she is, she is not bored. A part of her feels like the master of the universe.

So, what's the downside?

Pushing the limits of how much we can do is exhilarating. However, doing too much too fast can be exhausting, misguided, and potentially dangerous — for instance, cell phones while driving. In our overloaded world, time and attention can be depleted before the day's work has even begun. The quality of our work diminishes with speed. The faster you do something, the less well you do it.

The human form of life is meant for liberation, but unfortunately, due to the influence of Kali-yuga, every day the grhasthas are working hard like asses. Early in the morning they rise and travel even a hundred miles away to earn bread. Especially in the Western countries, I have seen that people awaken at five o'clock to go to offices and factories to earn their livelihood. People in Calcutta and Bombay also do this every day. They work very hard in the office or factory, and again they spend three or four hours in transportation returning home. Then they retire at ten o'clock and again rise early in the morning to go to their offices and factories. This kind of hard labor is described in the sastras as the life of pigs and stool-eaters. Nayam deho deha-bhajam nrloke kastan kaman arhate vid-bhujam ye: [SB 5.5.1] "Of all living entities who have accepted material bodies in this world, one who has been awarded this human form should not work hard day and night simply for sense gratification, which is available even for dogs and hogs that eat stool." (SB 5.5.1) One must find some time for hearing Srimad-Bhagavatam and Bhagavad-gita. This is Vedic culture. One should work eight hours at the most to earn his livelihood, ~ Srila Prabhupada (Srimad Bhagavatam 7.14.3-4)

When you're up, you ride this fast life like a surfer atop a great wave, but when you're down you wipe out.

Could you explain the "C-state" and the "F-state," and talk about that critical moment in-between?

You are in the "C-state" when your performance is effective and your temper is even: you feel calm, cool or collected. When your performance is ineffective and your temper unpleasant, you are in the "F-state": feeling frenzied, frustrated or flustered.

We often move from one state to another without realizing that these two states are separated by a precious interlude of warning. To acquire the skill of identifying the interlude when you're in it, all you have to do is know that it exists.

During the interlude, if you listen, you will say to yourself: "I'm about to lose it." Don't take the bait: back away, go outside, take a break. Listening to that voice can save a career, a marriage, or at least a day.

Is "time management" or "attention management" the goal?

Most current advice related to the problem of modern life focuses on the need to get organized. While disorganization is an important problem, it is not the root of the matter. You can be very well organized and still feel overwhelmed by modern life. There is so much you must do each day, and on top of that so much you could do, that your attention can be split and head off in many directions at once, like water from a garden hose whose nozzle has been set on wide spray. Instead, it is best to set your nozzle on jet stream. Focus your attention in one direction with full force.

You "pay with your attention." The idiom "to pay attention" has never been more apt, because the cost of your attention has never been this high. The cost is all that you must deny your attention — a dizzying list of other readily available targets. We are seduced, tantalized, and subliminally redirected by extraneous stimuli. People become victims of their own enthusiasm. All you have to do is get on to Google and in seconds you've found 23 things you want to do. We must train ourselves to stay on task as much as the world is training you to go off task.

What is the value of accepting limits?

You are far less likely to "get into trouble" if you accept limits. This concept is obvious with things like food and alcohol; we understand that when we eat or drink too much we put ourselves at risk. The risks are less obvious with commitments — but equally as dangerous. Know that keeping track of everything is impossible and having enough time to please everyone is equally impossible. Be careful not to over commit.

Early in my career, I learned that I had a maximum. As time went on I gained skill, my maximum increased, but there was always a maximum beyond which I could not work well. I learned to sense

---

Prajapati: It is considered one of our major problems, leisure time. People are having more time on their hands and they do not know what to do with it. So the government, they're scratching their heads inventing things for people to waste their time.

Prabhupada: This is the difficulty. Na te viduh svartha-gatim hi visnum [SB 7.5.31]. Because they are rascal, they do not know how to utilize time, what is the aim of life, where you have to go. These things they don't know. So they must waste time. So it is the... Just like child. He wastes time in so many ways. It is the duty of the parents, guardians, to cr..., synchronize his activities so that he may not waste his time. It is the duty of the guardians. Similarly these rascals, they're wasting time. You have to engage them in Krsna consciousness. Then their time will be utilized.

(Morning Walk -- January 5, 1974, Los Angeles)

---

when I reached it. I learned that if I let the job control me, if I responded to every request immediately, I was doomed. If I took control, let my instincts, knowledge and experience guide me and followed a plan, then I could get the job done well.

Do you have suggestions for gaining control?

The great trap for overachieving populations, such as Stanford's, is the illusion of not having control. I know the first thing I would hear from many of your readers is: "I understand the principles, but I have no choice. My boss, my work, my family demand it." I would respond by saying, "You have more control than you think." You will get your more important work done if you realize how much control you give away when you make yourself available to others on a 24/7 on-call basis — a boundary that is far too porous.

Words of advice?

You must choose. You must prioritize. In order to do well and be happy, you must say, to many people and activities, "No, thank you." In this era, you must deliberately preserve and cultivate your most valuable connections to people, activities and whatever else is most important to you. As you take back control and lead a sane life, you become the person you really want to be. You will enjoy — while they last — the childhoods of your kids, the ripening of your marriage, and these best years of your life. You will give yourself permission to make the most of the short time you have on this planet.

When we approach some gentleman and request him to become a reader of "Back to Godhead," sometimes we are replied to with the words "NO TIME." They say that they are too busy earning money for maintaining the body and soul together. But when we ask them what they mean by the "soul," they have nothing to reply.... But everybody should know from the Bhagavat Geeta that the body is the outward dress.... So if the dress is taken care of only, without any care of the real person -- it is sheer foolishness and a waste of time.

~ Srila Prabhupada (Back To Godhead)

Steps You Can Take

Disconnect

Don't always be connected. If you carry around an iPhone or Blackberry or other mobile device, shut it off. Better yet, learn to leave it behind when possible. If you work on a computer most of the day, have times when you disconnect so you can focus on other things. Being connected all the time means we're subject to interruptions, we're constantly stressed about information coming in, we are at the mercy of the demands of others. It's hard to slow down when you're always checking new messages coming in.

Appreciate Nature

Many of us are shut in our homes and offices and cars and trains most of the time, and rarely do we get the chance to go outside. And often even when people are outside, they're talking on their cell phones. Instead, take the time to go outside and really observe nature, take a deep breath of fresh air, enjoy the serenity of water and greenery. Exercise outdoors when you can, or find other outdoor activities to enjoy such as nature walks, hiking, swimming, etc. Feel the sensations of water and wind and earth against your skin. Try to do this daily — by yourself or with loved ones.

Eat slower

Instead of cramming food down our throats as quickly as possible — leading to overeating and a lack of enjoyment of our food — learn to eat slowly. Be mindful of each bite. Appreciate the flavors and textures. Eating slowly has the double benefit of making you fuller on less food and making the food taste better. Learn to eat more real food as well, with some great spices (instead of fat and salt and sugar and frying for flavor).

Drive Slower

Speedy driving is a pretty prevalent habit in our fast-paced world, but it's also responsible for a lot of traffic accidents, stress, and wasted fuel. Instead, make it a habit to slow down when you drive. Appreciate your surroundings. Make it a peaceful time to contemplate your life, and the things you're passing. Driving will be more enjoyable, and much safer. You'll use less fuel too.

Single-task

The opposite of multi-tasking. Focus on one thing at a time. When you feel the urge to switch to other tasks, pause, breathe, and pull yourself back. Increase your reading of print.

Breathe

When you find yourself speeding up and stressing out, pause, and take a deep breath. Take a couple more. Really feel the air coming into your body, and feel the stress going out. By fully focusing on each breath, you bring yourself back to the present, and slow yourself down. It's also nice to take a deep breath or two — do it now and see for yourself.

References:

David Backes, 5th May 2011

© Stanford University. BeWell @ Stanford Office

The 10 Essential Rules for Slowing Down and Enjoying Life More, Leo Babauta.

Slow Movements

The Slow Movement advocates a cultural shift toward slowing down life's pace. It began with Carlo Petrini's protest against the opening of a McDonald's restaurant in Piazza di Spagna, Rome in 1986 that sparked the creation of the Slow Food organization. Over time, this developed into a subculture in other areas, such as Slow Cities, Slow living, Slow Travel, and Slow Design.

Geir Berthelsen and his creation of The World Institute of Slowness presented a vision in 1999 for an entire 'Slow Planet' and a need to teach the world the way of Slow. Carl Honoré's 2004 book, In Praise of Slowness, first explored how the Slow philosophy might be applied in every field of human endeavour and coined the phrase "Slow Movement." The Financial Times said the book is "to the Slow Movement what Das Kapital is to communism."

Honoré describes the Slow Movement thus:

"It is a cultural revolution against the notion that faster is always better. The Slow philosophy is not about doing everything at a snail's pace. It's about seeking to do everything at the right speed. Savoring the hours and minutes rather than just counting them. Doing everything as well as possible, instead of as fast as possible. It's about quality over quantity in everything from work to food to parenting."

Professor Guttorm Fløistad summarizes the philosophy, stating: "The only thing for certain is that everything changes. The rate of change increases. If you want to hang on you better speed up. That is the message of today. It could however be useful to remind everyone that our basic needs never change. The need to be seen and appreciated! It is the need to belong. The need for nearness and care, and for a little love! This is given only through slowness in human relations. In order to master changes, we have to recover slowness, reflection and togetherness. There we will find real renewal."

The Slow Movement is not organized and controlled by a single organization. A fundamental characteristic of the Slow Movement is that it is propounded, and its momentum maintained, by individuals who constitute the expanding global community of Slow. Its popularity has grown considerably since the rise of Slow Food and Slow City in Europe, with Slow initiatives spreading as far as Australia and Japan.

Cittaslow (Slow City)

Cittaslow movement is to resist the homogenization and globalization of towns and cities. It seeks to improve the quality and enjoyment of living by encouraging happiness and self-determination.

Everything is going on. Your motorcar is going on. You are going on. We have a big city, especially in Europe, America, simply going on. This way, this... Whoosh, whoosh, whoosh. No rest. This is called jagat. Where he is going on? You have heard Rabindranath Tagore, poet Tagore. He wrote one article that "When I was in London I saw the people are walking very fast, the cars are going very fast. But I was thinking that 'This England is a small island; they may not fall down in the sea.' " (laughter) If you let loose your dog, it will go on this way, this way, this way, this way, this way. (laughter) This is jagat, going on. Going on, but condition: "You cannot go beyond this."
~ Srila Prabhupada (Lecture, Srimad-Bhagavatam 1.1.2 -- London, August 16, 1971)

Slow Art

Slow Art is an emerging movement evolving out of a philosophy of art and life expounded by the artist Tim Slowinski. It advocates appreciating an art work in itself as opposed to a rapid, flitting witnessing of art common in a hectic societal setting.

Another interpretation of Slow Art relates to creating art in a slow way. This practice is about being mindful of detail, valuing the history inherent in re-usable materials, putting time into creating small items. The practice encourages the maker to be naturally meditative as they create. "Slow" ends up being a way of being.

"I WANT YOU TO SLOW DOWN, AND THAT INCLUDES FAST FOOD."

Slow Church

Slow Church is a movement in Christian praxis which integrates Slow Movement principles into the structure and character of the local church. The phrase was introduced in 2008 by Christian bloggers working independently who imagined what such a "Slow Church" might look like. Over the next several years, the concept continued to be discussed online and in print by various writers and ministers.

In July 2012, a three-day conference titled Slow Church: Abiding Together in the Patient Work of God was held on the campus of DePaul University in Chicago on the topic of Slow Church.

Ethics, ecology, and economy are cited as areas of central concern to Slow Church. Slow Church is described as a "conversation" not a movement and has New Monasticism as an influence.

It has emphases on non-traditional ways for churches to operate and on "conversation" over dogma and hierarchy,

Slow Education

Slow education is based upon Socratic, adaptive and non-standards based approaches to teaching. Slow education is in part a reaction to the overly compacted course content requirements teachers are experiencing from nationalized curricula worldwide, which many educators find students cannot cover in a single year with sufficient depth. Slow education is also a reaction to the proliferation of standardized testing, favoring instead qualitative measures of student and teacher success.

"You're telling me it will take 13 years to install my education! What kind of outdated software is this school using?"

Slow education is frequently a feature in free, democratic and home schools. However, it can be a significant element in any classroom, including those in college preparatory and rigorous environments. The term "slow education" was derived from the distinction between slow food and fast food or junk food, and is an effort to associate quality, culture and personalization with quality schooling.

Slow Fashion

The term "Slow Fashion" was coined by Kate Fletcher in 2007 (Centre for Sustainable Fashion, UK). "Slow fashion is not a seasonal trend that comes and goes, but a sustainable fashion movement that is gaining momentum."

The Slow Fashion Movement is based on the same principles of the Slow Food Movement, as the alternative to mass-produced clothing (AKA "Fast-Fashion"). Initially, The Slow Clothing Movement was intended to reject all mass-produced clothing, referring only to clothing made by hand, but has broadened to include many interpretations and is practiced in various ways.

Some examples of slow fashion practices include:

Opposing and boycotting mass-produced fashion (AKA "Fast-Fashion" or "McFashion").

Choosing artisan products to support smaller businesses, fair trade and locally-made clothes.

Buying secondhand or vintage clothing and donating unwanted garments.

Choosing clothing made with sustainable, ethically-made or recycled fabrics.

Choosing quality garments that will last longer, transcend trends (a "classic" style), and be repairable.

Doing it yourself - making, mending, customizing, altering, and up-cycling your own clothing.

Slowing the rate of fashion consumption: buying fewer clothes less often.

The Slow Fashion movement is a unified representation of all the "sustainable", "eco", "green", and "ethical" fashion movements. It encourages education about the garment industry's connection and impact on the environment and depleting resources, slowing of the supply chain to reduce the number of trends and seasons, to encourage quality production, and return greater value to garments removing the image of disposability of fashion. A key phrase repeatedly heard in reference to Slow Fashion is "quality over quantity". This phrase is used to summarize the basic principles of slowing down the rate of clothing consumption by choosing garments that last longer.

Slow Food

Opposed to the culture of fast food, the sub-movement known as Slow Food seeks to encourage the enjoyment of regional produce, traditional foods, which are often grown organically and to enjoy these foods in the company of others. It aims to defend agricultural biodiversity.

The movement claims 83,000 members in 50 countries, which are organized into 800 Convivia or local chapters. Sometimes operating under a logo of a snail, the collective philosophy is to preserve and support traditional ways of life. Today, 42 states in the U.S. have their own convivium.

In 2004, representatives from food communities in more than 150 countries met in Turin under the umbrella of the Terra Madre (Mother Earth) network.

Slow Gardening

Slow Gardening is a movement that helps gardeners savor what they grow using all their senses through all the seasons. It is not about being lazy; rather it is aimed at getting more out of what they do.

" My doctor told me that I need to slow down,
but I don't think I can. "

Slow Goods

Slow Goods takes its core direction from various elements of the overall 'Slow Movement' and applying it to the concept, design and manufacturing of physical objects. It focuses on low production runs, the usage of craftspeople within the process and on-shore manufacturing. Proponents of this philosophy seek and collaborate with smaller, local supply and service partners.

Slow Goods practitioners must have those tenets baked into their business model, it must be the top driver in the procurement of sustainable materials and manufacturing techniques. The rationale for this local engagement facilitates the assurance of quality, the revitalization of local manufacturing industries and reduces greatly the footprint related to the shipment of goods across regions of land and or water.

This movement seeks to break current conventions of perpetuating the disposable nature of mass production. By using higher quality materials and craftsmanship, items attain a longer lifespan that harkens back to manufacturing golden era of the past.

Slow Media (Slow Television)

Slow Media is a movement aiming at sustainable and focused media production as well as media consumption. It formed in the context of a massive acceleration of news distribution ending in almost real-time digital media such as Twitter.

Followers experiment with a reduction of their daily media intake and log their efforts online ("Slow Media Diet").

Slow Money

Slow Money is a movement to organize investors and donors to steer new sources of capital to small food enterprises, organic farms, and local food systems. Slow Money takes its name from the Slow Food movement. Slow Money aims to develop the relationship between capital markets and place, including social and soil fertility.

Slow Parenting

Slow parenting encourages parents to plan less for their children, instead allowing them to enjoy their childhood and explore the world at their own pace. It is a response to hyper-parenting and 'helicopter' parenting, the widespread trend for parents to schedule activities and classes after school every day and every weekend, to solve problems on behalf of the children, and to buy services from commercial suppliers rather than letting nature take its course.

Last night we discussed about, that a dog is running from this side to that side. So he's feeling some pleasure. Similarly, we also, so-called civilized man, we are also running on a car, this side and this side. So the same thing -- the dog's race. But we are thinking, because we are running on a car, we are civilized. But the business is that dog's race. So Prahlada Maharaja's point is that we should try to understand the value of life. We should not waste our time by dog's race, either on four legs or on four wheels. That is the point. ~ Srila Prabhupada (Lecture Srimad-Bhagavatam 7.6.3 -- Toronto, June 19, 1976)

It was described most specifically by Carl Honoré in Under Pressure: Rescuing Our Children from the Culture Of Hyper-Parenting.

Slow Photography

Slow Photography is a term describing a tendency in today's contemporary Photography and Arts. In response to the spread of digital photography and the snapshot, artists and photographers retake manual techniques and working methods to work slower, manually and in constant dialogue with the physical materials of the images.

Slow Science

The Slow Science movement's objective is to enable scientists to take the time to think and read. The prevalent culture of science is publish or perish, where scientists are judged to be better if they publish more papers in less time, and only these who do so are able to maintain their careers. Those who practice and promote slow science suggest that "society should give scientists the time they need".

Slow Technology

Slow technology approach aims to emphasize that technology can support reflection rather than efficiency. This approach has been discussed through various examples, for example those in interaction design or virtual environments. It is related to other parallel efforts such as those towards reflective design, critical design and critical technical practice.

Slow Travel

Slow Travel is an evolving movement that has taken its inspiration from nineteenth-century European travel writers, such as Théophile Gautier, who reacted against the cult of speed, prompting some modern analysts to ask "If we have slow food and slow cities, then why not slow travel?".

Advocates of slow travel argue that all too often the potential pleasure of the journey is lost by too eager anticipation of arrival.

Slow travel, it is asserted, is a state of mind which allows travellers to engage more fully with communities along their route, often favouring visits to spots enjoyed by local residents rather than merely following guidebooks. As such, slow travel shares some common values with ecotourism. Its advocates and devotees generally look for low-impact travel styles, even to the extent of eschewing flying.

Aspects of slow travel, including some of the principles detailed in the Manifesto for Slow Travel, are now increasingly featuring in travel writing. The magazineHidden Europe, which published the Manifesto for Slow Travel, has particularly showcased slow travel, featuring articles that focus on unhurried, low-impact journeys and advocating a stronger engagement with communities that lie en route.

Slow down!
I wanna get there, but I wanna get there alive!

The International Institute of Not Doing Much (IINDM)

The International Institute of Not Doing Much (IINDM) is a humorous approach to the serious topic of time poverty, incivility, and workaholism. The Institute's fictional presence promotes counter-urgency. First created in 2005, SlowDownNow.org is a continually evolving work of art and humor which reports it has over 5,000 members.

References:

The World Institute of Slowness

Wikipedia

Kate Marie & Christopher Thomas (November 10, 2009). Fast Living Slow Ageing. Mileage Media. ISBN 9780980633900.

David Niven Miller. Growth Youthful.

Nunley, Jan (8 January 2008). "Slow Church". anglimergent. 1 March 2013.

Nunley, Jan (4 February 2008), ""Slow Church" Group Page", facebook.com, 1 March 2013

Childress, Kyle (20 May 2008). "Walking with God Slowly". 1 March 2013.

Land, Lucas (11 May 2009). "The Slow Church Movement". 1 March 2013.

Shellnutt, Kate (7 July 2011). "Slow food movement serves as church inspiration". Houston Chronicle. 1 March 2013.

McAteer, Anastasia and John (29 July 2011). "Slow Food, Slow Church". 1 March 2013.

Hauerwas, Stanley (6 July 2012). "Stan and Kyle Talk Slow Church". Slow Church: Abiding Together in the Patient Work of God. Interview with Kyle Childress. Chicago. 2 March 2013.

"Slow Church", facebook.com, 2 March 2013

"Slow Church", Patheos, 1 March 2013

C. Christopher Smith and John Pattison (2014). Slow Church. InterVarsity Press.

Smith, C. Christopher (December 2012). "Slow Down and Know That I Am God: Why it's time for a conversation about Slow Church". Sojourners. 1 March 2013.

Piatt, Christian (7 February 2013). "The Ikea Effect, Slow Church, and Laboring Our Way Into Love". Sojourners. 2 March 2013.

Journal for International Counselor Education 2012 Volume 4 , "Slow Counseling: Promoting Wellness in a Fast World"

Fashion:Tailoring a Strategic Approach Towards Sustainability by Maureen Dickson, Carlotta Cataldi, and Crystal Grover

What is Slow Fashion? by Jessica Bourland, Slow Fashioned

Creative Pause

The Upside of Downtime

For computers or machines, the term downtime is used to refer to periods when a their services are unavailable. Downtime or outage duration refers to a period of time that a system fails to provide or perform its primary function. The term is commonly applied to networks and servers.

But the term also applies to persons. Downtime is when there really isn't anything to do, at least not immediately. When you work in the office, workflow can sometimes become inconsistent. You will have busy times and you will have down times.

Employers and managers will expect employees to be working or at least keep busy with something. This is where you, as an employee, need to be proactive. If there is no immediate business to work on, then find something to do.

There's An Upside To Downtime

For one, creating the space for downtime increases productivity. Subject to heavy workloads and never-ending to-do lists, it's easy to put our heads down and charge through tasks, thinking we have no time for days off, free evenings, or weeklong vacations.

But driving too hard without breaks can make us less productive and less focused. One experiment conducted at BCG, for example, found that forcing employees to take days, nights, or extended periods of time off actually increased productivity. And other studies show that brief periods of downtime, like afternoon naps, can restore focus and energy.

Taking the time to get out of the details and view of the larger picture can also help us better understand the purpose and priority of our tasks. As Tony Schwartz has written, "human beings perform best and are most productive when they *alternate between periods of intense focus and intermittent renewal.*"

Similarly, employing downtime — on a planned and ad hoc basis — unleashes creativity. 3M is one of the most innovative companies in history, and to feed their innovation engine, the company introduced "15% time" back in 1948 — giving employees 15% downtime to pursue their own projects, a practice that has since been replicated at companies like Google.

Jonah Lehrer has written for The New Yorker about the virtue of daydreaming, and in his book 'Imagine' notes the necessity of downtime for problem solving, saying, "While it's commonly assumed that the best way to solve a difficult problem is to relentlessly focus, this clenched state of mind comes with a

I think once every 14 days. And I am the biggest thinker in America.
~ Mark Twain

hidden cost: it inhibits the sort of creative connections that lead to breakthroughs."

Finally, downtime can dramatically improve mental and physical health and our personal relationships. One study, for example, found that employees who unplugged and took time off reduced serious health issues like coronary heart disease.

Victor Lipman has written in Forbes that exercising midday can help to reduce workplace stress. As John has written previously, just six minutes of reading can reduce stress by 68%. John Tierney and Ron Baumeister state in Willpower that midday breaks can rejuvenate willpower and improve judgment and decision making in the afternoon.

And as we have written before, cleanly taking time off from work to focus on your spouse, family, or friends can only improve your relationships. Downtime can be essential for mental, physical, and social health.

Why Your Brain Needs More Downtime

Research on naps, meditation, nature walks and the habits of exceptional artists and athletes reveals how mental breaks increase productivity, replenish attention, solidify memories and encourage creativity

Ferris Jabr writes in Scientific American:

Every now and then during the workweek—usually around three in the afternoon—a familiar ache begins to saturate my forehead and pool in my temples. The glare of my computer screen appears to suddenly intensify. My eyes trace the contour of the same sentence two or three times, yet I fail to extract its meaning. Even if I began the day undaunted, getting through my ever growing list of stories to write and edit, e-mails to send and respond to, and documents to read now seems as futile as scaling a mountain that continuously thrusts new stone skyward. There is so much more to do—so much work I genuinely enjoy—but my brain is telling me to stop. It's full. It needs some downtime.

Meditation Marathon

Freelance writer and meditation teacher Michael Taft has experienced his own version of cerebral congestion. "In a normal working day in modern America, there's a sense of so much coming at you at once, so much to process that you just can't deal with it all," Taft says.

In 2011, while finalizing plans to move from Los Angeles to San Francisco, he decided to take an especially long recess from work and the usual frenzy of life. After selling his home and packing all his belongings in storage, he traveled to the small rural community of Barre, Mass., about 100 kilometers west of Boston, where every year people congregate for a three-month-long "meditation marathon."

Taft had been on similar retreats before, but never one this long. For 92 days he lived at Insight Meditation Society's Forest Refuge facility, never speaking a word to anyone else. He spent most of his time meditating, practicing yoga and walking through fields and along trails in surrounding farmland and woods, where he encountered rafters of turkeys leaping from branches, and once spotted an otter gamboling in a swamp.

Gradually, his mind seemed to sort through a backlog of unprocessed data and to empty itself of accumulated concerns. "When you go on a long retreat like that there's a kind of base level of mental tension and busyness that totally evaporates," Taft says. "I call that my 'mind being not full.' Currently, the speed of life doesn't allow enough interstitial time for things to just kind of settle down."

Many people in the U.S. and other industrialized countries would wholeheartedly agree with Taft's sentiments, even if they are not as committed to meditation.

A 2010 LexisNexis survey of 1,700 white collar workers in the U.S., China, South Africa, the U.K. and Australia revealed that on average employees spend more than half their workdays receiving and managing information rather than using it to do their jobs; half of the surveyed workers also confessed that they were reaching a breaking point after which they would not be able to accommodate the deluge of data.

In contrast to the European Union, which mandates 20 days of paid vacation, the U.S. has no federal laws guaranteeing paid time off, sick leave or even breaks for national holidays. In the Netherlands 26 days of vacation in a given year is typical. In America, Canada, Japan and Hong Kong workers average 10 days off each year. Yet a survey by Harris Interactive found that, at the end of 2012, Americans had an average of nine unused vacation days. And in several surveys Americans have admitted that they obsessively check and respond to e-mails from their colleagues or feel obliged to get some work done in between kayaking around the coast of Kauai and learning to pronounce humuhumunukunukuapua'a.

To summarize, Americans and their brains are preoccupied with work much of the time. Throughout history people have intuited that such puritanical devotion to perpetual busyness does not in fact translate to greater productivity and is not particularly healthy.

What if the brain requires substantial downtime to remain industrious and generate its most innovative ideas? "Idleness is not just a vacation, an indulgence or a vice; it is as indispensable to the brain as vitamin D is to the body, and deprived of it we suffer a mental affliction as disfiguring as rickets," essayist Tim Kreider wrote in The New York Times. "The space and quiet that idleness provides is a necessary condition for standing back from life and seeing it whole, for making unexpected connections and waiting for the wild summer lightning strikes of inspiration—it is, paradoxically, necessary to getting any work done."

'Overwhelming' Amount Of Empirical Evidence

In making an argument for the necessity of mental downtime, we can now add an overwhelming amount of empirical evidence to intuition and anecdote. Why giving our brains a break now and then is so important has become increasingly clear in a diverse collection of new studies investigating: the habits of office workers and the daily routines of extraordinary musicians and athletes; the benefits of vacation, meditation and time spent in parks, gardens and other peaceful outdoor spaces; and how napping, unwinding while awake and perhaps the mere act of blinking can sharpen the mind.

What research to date also clarifies, however, is that even when we are relaxing or daydreaming, the brain does not really slow down or stop working. Rather—just as a dazzling array of molecular, genetic and physiological processes occur primarily or even exclusively when we sleep at night—many important mental processes seem to require what we call downtime and other forms of rest during the day. Downtime replenishes the brain's stores of attention and motivation, encourages productivity and creativity, and is essential to both achieve our highest levels of performance and simply form stable memories in everyday life. A wandering mind unsticks us in time so that we can learn from the past and plan for the future. Moments of respite may even be necessary to keep one's moral compass in working order and maintain a sense of self.

In a recent thought-provoking review of research on the default mode network (DMN), Mary Helen Immordino-Yang of the University of Southern California and her co-authors argue that when we are resting the brain is anything but idle and that, far from being purposeless or unproductive, downtime is in fact essential to mental processes that affirm our identities, develop our understanding of human behavior and instill an internal code of ethics—processes that depend on the DMN.

Downtime is an opportunity for the brain to make sense of what it has recently learned, to surface fundamental unresolved tensions in our lives and to swivel its powers of reflection away from the external world toward itself. While mind-wandering we replay conversations we had earlier that day, rewriting our verbal blunders as a way of learning to avoid them in the future. We craft fictional dialogue to practice standing up to someone who intimidates us or to reap the satisfaction of an imaginary harangue against someone who wronged us. We shuffle through all those neglected mental post-it notes listing half-finished projects and we mull over the aspects of our lives with which we are most dissatisfied, searching for solutions.

We sink into scenes from childhood and catapult ourselves into different hypothetical futures. And we subject ourselves to a kind of moral performance review, questioning how we have treated others lately. These moments of introspection are also one way we form a sense of self, which is essentially a story we continually tell ourselves.

When it has a moment to itself, the mind dips its quill into our memories, sensory experiences, disappointments and desires so that it may continue writing this ongoing first-person narrative of life.

Related research suggests that the default mode network is more active than is typical in especially creative people, and some studies have demonstrated that the mind obliquely solves tough problems while daydreaming—an experience many people have had while taking a shower.

"I'm learning how to relax, doctor—but I want to relax better and faster! I WANT TO BE ON THE CUTTING EDGE OF RELAXATION!"

Epiphanies may seem to come out of nowhere, but they are often the product of unconscious mental activity during downtime. In a

Downtime for systems – a bad thing. Downtime for people – priceless. OK, it's an overused line, but true none the less. After well over a year with no serious vacation, I spent the past week and a half with family in mid-west. A week on the shore of Lake Eerie boating with the kids and setting off a few hundred dollars worth of fireworks (something we can't do in California). With the exception of a couple dozen mosquito souveniers it was just the battery recharge I needed.

~ Barmijo — July 12, 2007

2006 study, Ap Dijksterhuis and his colleagues asked 80 University of Amsterdam students to pick the best car from a set of four that—unbeknownst to the students—the researchers had previously ranked based on size, mileage, maneuverability and other features. Half the participants got four minutes to deliberate after reviewing the specs; the researchers prevented the other 40 from pondering their choices by distracting them with anagrams. Yet the latter group made far better decisions. Solutions emerge from the subconscious in this way only when the distracting task is relatively simple, such as solving an anagram or engaging in a routine activity that does not necessitate much deliberate concentration, like brushing one's teeth or washing dishes.

With the right kind of distraction the default mode network may be able to integrate more information from a wide range of brain regions in more complex ways than when the brain is consciously working through a problem.

During downtime, the brain also concerns itself with more mundane but equally important duties. For decades scientists have suspected that when an animal or person is not actively learning something new, the brain consolidates recently accumulated data, memorizing the most salient information, and essentially rehearses recently learned skills, etching them into its tissue. Most of us have observed how, after a good night's sleep, the vocab words we struggled to remember the previous day suddenly leap into our

---

Now, one child may like to play with a motorcar toy, another with a doll, and so on. And the parents are supplying: "All right, you take this toy car, you take this doll." Similarly, we are playing like that—making plans to enjoy—and God is supplying all our necessities. But He doesn't want to do that. He says, "My dear child, you are grown up now; you have this human body. Don't play like this and waste your time. Get an education and know things as they are." That education is called brahma-jijnasa, "inquiry into the Absolute Truth."

~ Srila Prabhupada (The Human Machine)

---

minds or that technically challenging piano song is much easier to play. *Dozens of studies have confirmed that memory depends on sleep.* A tantalizing piece of evidence suggests that the brain may take advantage of every momentary lapse in attention to let resting state networks take over.

All In A Day's Work

That learning and memory depend on both sleep and waking rest may partially explain why some of the most exceptional artists and athletes among us fall into a daily routine of intense practice punctuated by breaks and followed by a lengthy period of recuperation. Psychologist K. Anders Ericsson of The Florida State University has spent more than 30 years studying how people achieve the highest levels of expertise.

Based on his own work and a thorough review of the relevant research, Ericsson has concluded that most people can engage in deliberate practice—which means pushing oneself beyond current limits—for only an hour without rest; that extremely talented people in many different disciplines—music, sports, writing—rarely practice more than four hours each day on average; and that many experts prefer to begin training early in the morning when mental and physical energy is readily available. "Unless the daily levels of practice are restricted, such that subsequent rest and nighttime sleep allow the individuals to restore their equilibrium," Ericsson wrote, "individuals often encounter overtraining injuries and, eventually, incapacitating 'burnout.'"

These principles are derived from the rituals of the exceptional, but they are useful for just about anyone in any profession, including typical nine-to-fivers. Corporate America may never sanction working only four hours a day, but research suggests that to maximize productivity we should reform the current model of consecutive 40-hour workweeks separated only by two-day weekends and sometimes interrupted by short vacations.

Psychologists have established that vacations have real benefits. Vacations likely revitalize the body and mind by distancing people from job-related stress; by immersing people in new places, cuisines and social circles, which in turn may lead to original ideas and insights; and by giving people the opportunity to get a good night's sleep and to let their minds drift from one experience to the next, rather than forcing their brains to concentrate on a single task for hours at a time.

But a recent comprehensive meta-analysis by Jessica de Bloom, now at the University of Tampere in Finland, demonstrates that these benefits generally fade within two to four weeks. In one of de Bloom's own studies 96 Dutch workers reported feeling more energetic, happier, less tense and more satisfied with their lives than usual during a winter sports vacation between seven and nine days long. Within one week of returning to work, however, all the feelings of renewal dissipated. A second experiment on four and five days of respite came to essentially the same conclusion. A short vacation is like a cool shower on an oppressively muggy summer day—a refreshing yet fleeting escape.

Instead of limiting people to a single weeklong vacation each year or a few three-day vacations here and there, companies should also allow their employees to take a day or two off during the workweek and encourage workers to banish all work-related tasks from their evenings.

In a four-year study, Leslie Perlow of the Harvard Business School and her colleagues tracked the work habits of employees at the Boston Consulting Group. Each year they insisted that employees take regular time off, even when they did not think they should be away from the office. In one experiment each of five consultants on a team took a break from work one day a week.

In a second experiment every member of a team scheduled one weekly night of uninterrupted personal time, even though they were accustomed to working from home in the evenings.

Everyone resisted at first, fearing they would only be postponing work. But over time the consultants learned to love their scheduled time off because it consistently replenished their willingness and ability to work, which made them more productive overall.

After five months employees experimenting with deliberate periodic rest were more satisfied with their jobs, more likely to envision a long-term future at the company, more content with their work–life balance and prouder of their accomplishments.

Tony Schwartz, a journalist and CEO of The Energy Project, has made a career out of teaching people to be more productive by changing the way they think about downtime.

His strategy relies in part on the idea that anyone can learn to regularly renew their

—GLASBERGEN

"I spent the afternoon digesting my lunch, pumping several quarts of blood through miles of tissue, filtering toxins in my liver, and replacing millions of skin cells. I didn't have time for anything else."

reservoirs of physical and mental energy. "People are working so many hours that not only in most cases do they not have more hours they could work, but there's also strong evidence that when they work for too long they get diminishing returns in terms of health costs and emotional costs," Schwartz says. "If time is no longer an available resource, what is? The answer is energy."

Schwartz and his colleagues encourage workers to get seven to eight hours of sleep every night, to use all their vacation days, take power naps and many small breaks during the day, practice meditation, and tackle the most challenging task first thing in the morning so they can give it their full attention. "Many things we are suggesting are in some ways very simple and on some level are things people already knew, but they are moving at such extraordinary speed that they have convinced themselves they are not capable of those behaviors," Schwartz says.

The Energy Project's approach was a tough sell at first—because it contradicts the prevailing ethos that busier is better—but the organization has so far successfully partnered with Google, Apple, Facebook, Coca-Cola, Green Mountain Coffee, Ford, Genentech and a wide range of Fortune 500 companies. To gauge how employees improve over time, Schwartz measures their level of engagement—that is, how much they like their jobs and are willing to go above and beyond their basic duties—a trait that many studies have correlated with performance. Admittedly, this is not the most precise or direct measurement, but Schwartz says that time and again his strategies have pushed workers' overall engagement well above the average level and that Google has been satisfied enough to keep up the partnership for more than five years.

Put Your Mind At Rest

Many recent studies have corroborated the idea that our mental resources are continuously depleted throughout the day and that various kinds of rest and downtime can both replenish those reserves and increase their volume. Consider, for instance, how even an incredibly brief midday nap enlivens the mind.

By adulthood, most of us have adopted the habit of sleeping through the night and staying awake for most or all of the day—but this may not be ideal for our mental health and is certainly not the only way people have slept throughout history.

In somewhat the same way that hobbits in Tolkien's Middle Earth enjoy a first and second breakfast, people living without electricity in preindustrial Europe looked forward to a first and second sleep divided by about an hour of crepuscular activity. During that hour, they would pray, relieve themselves, may be smoke and even visit neighbors.

Some researchers have proposed that people are also physiologically inclined to snooze during a 2 P.M. to 4 P.M. "nap zone"—or what some might call the afternoon slump—because the brain prefers to toggle between sleep and wake more than once a day.

As far back as the first century B.C. the Romans regularly took midafternoon breaks, which they called *meridiari* from the Latin for midday. Under the influence of Roman Catholicism, noon became known as sexta (the sixth hour, according to their clocks), a time for rest and prayer. Eventually sexta morphed into siesta.

Plenty of studies have established that naps sharpen concentration and improve the performance of both the sleep-deprived and the fully rested on all kinds of tasks, from driving to medical care. A 2004 study, for example, analyzed four years of data on highway car accidents involving Italian policemen and concluded that the practice of napping before night shifts reduced the prospective number of collisions by 48 percent.

In a 2002 study by Rebecca Smith-Coggins of Stanford University and her colleagues, 26 physicians and nurses working three consecutive 12-hour night shifts napped for 40 minutes at 3 A.M. while 23 of their colleagues worked continuously without sleeping. Although doctors and nurses that had napped scored lower than their peers on a memory test at 4 A.M., at 7:30 A.M. they outperformed the no-nap group on a test of attention, more efficiently inserted a catheter in a virtual simulation and were more alert during an interactive simulation of driving a car home.

Long naps work great when people have enough time to recover from "sleep inertia"—post-nap grogginess that, in some cases, can take more than two hours to fade. In other situations micronaps may be a smarter strategy.

We learn from the book Sanat Sujātēya that four things are required in attaining perfection in yoga practice: 1) the scriptures; 2) enthusiasm; 3) a bona fide spiritual master; 4) sufficient time.
~ Srila Prabhupada (RTW 5.1: The Highest Use of Intelligence)

An intensive 2006 study by Amber Brooks and Leon Lack of Flinders University in Australia and their colleagues pitted naps of five, 10, 20 and 30 minutes against one another to find out which was most restorative. Over a span of three years 24 college students periodically slept for only five hours on designated nights. The day after each of those nights they visited the lab to nap and take tests of attention that required them to respond quickly to images on a screen, complete a word search and accurately copy sequences of arcane symbols.

A five-minute nap barely increased alertness, but naps of 10, 20 and 30 minutes all improved the students' scores. But volunteers that napped 20 or 30 minutes had to wait half an hour or more for their sleep inertia to wear off before regaining full alertness, whereas 10-minute naps immediately enhanced performance just as much as the longer naps without any grogginess.

Although some start-ups and progressive companies provide their employees with spaces to nap at the office, most workers in the corporate world do not have that option. An equally restorative and likely far more manageable solution to mental fatigue is spending more time outdoors—in the evenings, on the weekends and even during lunch breaks by walking to a nearby park, riverfront or anywhere not dominated by skyscrapers and city streets.

Marc Berman, a psychologist at the University of South Carolina and a pioneer of a relatively new field called ecopsychology, argues that whereas *the hustle and bustle of a typical city taxes our attention, natural environments restore it.*

Contrast the experience of walking through Times Square in New York City—where the brain is ping-ponged between neon lights, honking taxies and throngs of tourists—with a day hike in a nature reserve, where the mind is free to leisurely shift its focus from the calls of songbirds to the gurgling and gushing of rivers to sunlight falling through every gap in the tree branches and puddling on the forest floor.

In one of the few controlled ecopsychology experiments, Berman asked 38 University of Michigan students to study lists of random numbers and recite them from memory in reverse order before completing another attention-draining task in which they memorized the locations of certain words arranged in a grid. Half the students subsequently strolled along a predefined path in an arboretum for about an hour whereas the other half walked the same distance through highly trafficked streets of downtown Ann Arbor for the same period of time.

Back at the lab the students memorized and recited digits once again. On average, volunteers that had ambled among trees recalled 1.5 more digits than the first time they took the test; those who had walked through the city improved by only 0.5 digits—a small but statistically significant difference between the two groups.

Beyond renewing one's powers of concentration, downtime can in fact bulk up the muscle of attention—something that scientists have observed repeatedly in studies on meditation. There are almost as many varieties and definitions of meditation as there are people who practice it. Although meditation is not equivalent to zoning out or daydreaming, many styles challenge people to sit in a quiet space, close their eyes and turn their attention away from the outside world toward their own minds. Mindfulness meditation, for example, generally refers to a sustained focus on one's thoughts, emotions and sensations in the present moment. For many people, mindfulness is about paying close attention to whatever the mind does on its own, as opposed to directing one's mind to accomplish this or that.

Mindfulness training has become more popular than ever in the last decade as a strategy to relieve stress, anxiety and depression.

Many researchers acknowledge that studies on the benefits of mindfulness often lack scientific rigor, use too few participants and rely too heavily on people's subjective reports, but at this point they have gathered enough evidence to conclude that meditation can indeed improve mental health, hone one's ability to concentrate and strengthen memory. Studies comparing long-time expert meditators with novices or people who do not meditate often find that the former outperform the latter on tests of mental acuity.

In a 2009 study, for example, Sara van Leeuwen of Johann Wolfgang Goethe University in Germany and her colleagues tested the visual attention of three groups of volunteers: 17 adults around 50 years old with up to 29 years of meditation practice; 17 people of the same age and gender who were not longtime meditators; and another 17 young adults who had never meditated before. In the test, a series of random letters flashed on a computer screen, concealing two digits in their midst. Volunteers had to identify both numerals and to guess if they did not glimpse one in time; recognizing the second number is often difficult because earlier images mask it.

Performance on such tests usually declines with age, but the expert meditators outscored both their peers and the younger participants.

Improve this mode of life. Live in open place, produce your food grains, produce your milk, save time, chant Hare Krsna. Plain living, high thinking, ideal life. Artificial necessities of life do increase your so-called comforts, but if you forget your real business, that is suicidal. We want to stop this suicidal policy. We don't want to stop the modern advancement of technology, although the so-called advancement technology is suicidal. But we don't talk of this. (laughter) Chaitanya Mahaprabhu has therefore given a simple formula -- chant Hare Krsna. Even in your technological factories, you can chant. What is the wrong there? You go on with operating your machine and chant, Hare Krsna, Hare Krsna, Krsna Krsna Hare Hare.
~ Srila Prabhupada (Room Conversation, New Vrindavan, June 24, 1976)

Heleen Slagter of Leiden University in Amsterdam and her colleagues used the same type of attention test in a 2007 study to compare 17 people who had just completed a three-month meditation retreat in Barre, Mass., with 23 mindfulness-curious volunteers who were meditating around 20 minutes a day. Both groups were evenly matched before their training, but when the retreat was over the meditation marathoners trumped the novices. Judging by recordings from an electroencephalogram, 90 days of meditation likely made the brain more efficient, so that it used up less available attention to successfully complete the test.

Rather profound changes to the brain's structure and behavior likely underlie many of these improvements. Numerous studies have shown that meditation strengthens connections between regions of the default mode network, for example, and can help people learn to more effectively shift between the DMN and circuits that are most active when we are consciously fixated on a task.

Over time expert meditators may also develop a more intricately wrinkled cortex—the brain's outer layer, which is necessary for many of our most sophisticated mental abilities, like abstract thought and introspection. Meditation appears to increase the volume and density of the hippocampus, a seahorse-shaped area of the brain that is absolutely crucial for memory; it thickens regions of the frontal cortex that we rely on to rein in our emotions; and it stymies the typical wilting of brain areas responsible for sustaining attention as we get older.

Just how quickly meditation can noticeably change the brain and mind is not yet clear. But a handful of experiments suggest that a couple weeks of meditation or a mere 10 to 20 minutes of mindfulness a day can whet the mind—if people stick with it. Likewise, a few studies indicate that meditating daily is ultimately more important than the total hours of meditation over one's lifetime.

In a 2007 study by Richard Chambers of the University of Melbourne, 40 people between the ages of 21 and 63 took various tests of attention and working memory, a collection of mental talents that allow someone to temporarily store and manipulate information. Half the volunteers completed the tests immediately before participating in an intensive 10-day meditation course—something they had never done before—and took the same tests again seven to 10 days after the course ended. The other half also took the tests on two occasions 21 days apart but did not practice any meditation. Whereas people who meditated performed quite a bit

"If you hire me to bark at your employees, that will free you for more important things."

better on the tests the second time around, those who did not meditate showed no meaningful improvement.

Similarly, in a 2007 study, 40 Chinese college students scored higher on attention tests after a mere 20 minutes of mindfulness-related meditation a day for five days, whereas 40 of their peers who did not meditate did not improve. And as little as 12 minutes of mindfulness meditation a day helped prevent the stress of military service from deteriorating the working memory of 34 U.S. marines in a 2011 study conducted by Amishi Jha, now at the University of Miami, and her colleagues.

"When people in the military have a gym they will work out in the gym. When they are on the side of a mountain they will make do with what they have and do push-ups to stay in shape," Jha says. "Mindfulness training may offer something similar for the mind. It's low-tech and easy to implement." In her own life, Jha looks for any and all existing opportunities to practice mindfulness, such as her 15-minute trip to and from work each day.

Likewise, Michael Taft advocates deliberate mental breaks during "all the in-between moments" in an average day—a subway ride, lunch, a walk to the bodega. He stresses, though, that there's a big difference between admiring the idea of more downtime and committing to it in practice. "Getting out into nature on the weekends, meditating, putting away our computers now and then—a lot of it is stuff we already know we should probably do," he says. "But we have to be a lot more diligent about it. Because it really does matter."

References:

Staffing Advice, From Millennium Personnel Corp.

Jackie Coleman and John Coleman, December, 2012

Scientific American, Ferris Jabr, October 2013

The Extinction of Deep Thinking & Sacred Space

Disconnecting From The Digital World Means Connecting To Ourselves

Interruption-free space is sacred. Yet, in the digital era we live in, we are losing hold of the few sacred spaces that remain untouched by email, the internet, people, and other forms of distraction. Our cars now have mobile phone integration and a thousand satellite radio stations. When walking from one place to another, we have our devices streaming data from dozens of sources. Even at our bedside, we now have our iPads with heaps of digital apps and the world's information at our fingertips.

There has been much discussion about the value of the "creative pause" – a state described as "the shift from being fully engaged in a creative activity to being passively engaged, or the shift to being disengaged altogether." This phenomenon is the seed of the break-through moments that people so frequently report having in the shower. In these moments, you are completely isolated, and your mind is able to wander and churn big questions without interruption.

However, despite the incredible power and potential of sacred spaces, they are quickly becoming extinct. We are depriving ourselves of every opportunity for disconnection. And our imaginations suffer the consequences.

Why Do We Crave Distraction Over Downtime?

Why do we give up our sacred space so easily? Because space is scary. During these temporary voids of distraction, our minds return to the uncertainty and fears that plague all of us. To escape this chasm of self-doubt and unanswered questions, you tune into all of the activity and data for reassurance.

But this desperate need for constant connection and stimulation is not a modern problem. We have always sought a state of constant connection from the dawn of time, but the way it is being done now is the problem,

We are depriving ourselves of every opportunity for disconnection. The need to be connected is, in fact, very basic in Maslow's hierarchy of needs, the psychological theory that explains the largest and most fundamental human desires. Our need for a sense of belonging comes right after physical safety. We thrive on friendship, family, and the constant affirmation of our

Hog civilization. We are restricting that "Don't work hard like hog and dog or animals, just satisfy your minimal necessities of life, save time and pursue spiritual understanding. This is our mission. Their mission is, "What is this nonsense, spiritual understanding? Simply some sentiment, waste of time. Produce, enjoy, invent so many things for sense gratification." Western civilization. And this is very attractive to the raksasa class. Eat, drink, be merry and enjoy. This is the raksasa mentality. As soon as there is television, or similar invention, they become very much enthused. They purchase and sitting down, they waste their time. I have seen in America the old man of family, one dog, one television, simply wasting time.

~ *Srila Prabhupada (Morning Walk -- January 6, 1976, Bombay)*

existence and relevance. Our self-esteem is largely a product of our interactions with others.

But today our craving to always feel loved and cared for is supplied by the "comment walls" on Facebook. Our confidence and self-esteem are judged by the number of "followers" on Twitter or the number of "likes" garnered by your photographs and blog posts.

So what's the solution? How do we reclaim our sacred spaces?

"Aside from ulcers, heart attacks, bypass surgery, drug and alcohol problems, and broken families, a little hard work never hurt anyone!"

Soon enough, planes, trains, subways, and, yes, showers will offer the option of staying connected. Knowing that we cannot rely on spaces that force us to unplug to survive much longer, we must be proactive in creating these spaces for ourselves. And when we have a precious opportunity to NOT be connected, we should develop the capacity to use it and protect it.

Here are five potential mindsets and solutions for consideration:

1. Rituals For Unplugging.

Perhaps those in biblical times knew what was in store for us when they created the Sabbath? The notion of a day every week reserved for reflection has become more important than ever

> *I feel blessed to live in a town that that is rates as having 30 electricity black outs a month. Love the down time this creates. Out of office walks, candle lit dinners, early bed times, cookies and kids, meaningful conversations, alone time and quality together time...time to think....time spent outside with the farm animals, time to garden without a guilty conscience, time to say..."Great! Another power cut!"*
> *~ Gamen Rasove*

before. It's about more than just refraining from work. It's about unplugging. The recent Sabbath Manifesto movement has received mainstream, secular accolades for the concept of ritualizing the period of disconnection. Perhaps you will reserve one day on the weekend where you force yourself to disconnect? At first, such efforts will feel very uncomfortable. You will deal with a bout of "connection withdrawal," but stay with it.

2. Daily Doses Of Deep Thinking.

Perhaps "sacred space" is a new life tenet that we must adopt in the 21st century? Since we know that unplugging will only become more difficult over time, we will need to develop a discipline for ourselves. Back in the day when the TV became a staple of every American home, parents started mandating time for their children to read. "TV time" became a controlled endeavor because, otherwise, it would consume every waking moment. Now, every waking moment is "connected time," and we need to start controlling it.

We need some rules. When it comes to scheduling, we will need to allocate blocks of time for deep thinking. Maybe you will carve out a 1-2 hour block on your calendar every day for taking a walk or just pondering some of those bigger things. *I can even imagine a day*

You are trying to get the unlimited happiness and you are not prepared to sacrifice anything? What is that sacrifice? You have to sacrifice little time. Come here and hear this Bhagavad-gita and chant with us. Is it very great sacrifice? And you will learn everything. Just to sacrifice little time. In former days they used to sacrifice their whole life for realizing self-realization. Deva-munindra-guhyam. Even the demigods, even great saintly persons, they sacrificed everything; still, they were unsuccessful. You see? Now, for this age, Lord Chaitanya mercifully has given you so much easier process for God realization. There is no comparison. Simply to sacrifice a little time. Sravanam. Simply hear. You haven't got to pay any charges. Sravanam. Simply you have to sit down a little patiently and hear.

~ Srila Prabhupada (Lecture, Bhagavad-gita 9.11-14 -- New York, November 27, 1966)

when homes and apartments have a special switch that shuts down wi-fi and data access during dinner or at night – just to provide a temporary pause from the constant flow of status updates and other communications.

3. Meditation And Naps To Clear The Mind.

There is no better mental escape from our tech-charged world than the act of meditation. If only for 15 minutes, the ability to steer your mind away from constant stimulation is downright liberating. There are various kinds of meditation. Some forms require you to think about nothing and completely clear your mind. (This is quite hard, at least for me.) Other forms of meditation are about focusing on one specific thing – often your breath, or a mantra that you repeat in your head (or out loud) for 10-15 minutes. At first, any sort of meditation might feel like a chore.

TAKING IT EASY IS HARD.

But with practice, it will become an energizing exercise.

If you can't adopt meditation, you might also try clearing your mind the old fashioned way – by sleeping. The legendary energy expert and bestselling author Tony Schwartz takes a 20-minute nap every day. Even if it's a few hours before he presents to a packed audience, he'll take a short nap. I asked him how he overcomes the midday anxiety enough to nap. His trick? "Practice," he said. Like all skills that don't come naturally, practice makes perfect.

4. Protect The State Of No-Intent.

When you're rushing to a solution, your mind will jump to the easiest and most familiar path. But when you allow yourself to just look out the window for 10 minutes – and ponder – your brain will start working in a more creative way. It will grasp ideas from unexpected places. It's this very sort of unconscious creativity that leads to great thinking. When you're driving or showering, you're letting your mind wander because you don't have to focus on anything in particular. If you do carve out some time for unobstructed thinking, be sure to free yourself from any specific intent.

5. Brilliance In 21st Century

The potential of our own creativity is rapidly being compromised by the era we live in. I believe that genius in the 21st century will be attributed to people who are able to unplug from the constant state of reactionary workflow, reduce their amount of insecurity work, and allow their minds to solve the great challenges of our era. Brilliance is so rare because it is always obstructed, often by the very stuff that keeps us so busy.

Reference

by Scott Belsky

Scott Belsky is Adobe's Vice President of Community and Co-Founder & Head of Behance, the leading online platform for creatives to showcase and discover creative work.

February 18

Gather Tidbits

Every Penny Makes A Million

And Every Drop An Ocean

R alph Waldo Emerson says "Guard well your spare moments. They are like uncut diamonds. Discard them and their value will never be known. Improve them and they will become the brightest gems in a useful life."

From client meetings to dentist appointments, it's impossible to avoid waiting for someone or something. But you don't need to just sit there and twiddle your thumbs. Always take something to do with you.

Turning Wait Time Into Productive Time

We've all been there…..

You show up at the doctor's office on time, only to discover that they're running behind and four others with appointments ahead of you are still waiting.

Or the airport where you wait for hours, only to hear the announcement that your delayed flight has been rescheduled – again.

Or the "quick visit" to the post office that drags on for an hour.

And if you are a parent… well, you probably have "scheduled" wait times built into your calendar – soccer practice, swim lessons, piano classes…When you are busy and stressed, even a short wait feels like eternity. Every minute that you wait, is a minute wasted.

"Wait time" can be the most frustrating time – if you let it. With just a little bit of planning though, you can not only turn "wait time" into productive time, but may actually surprise yourself by looking forward to it!

Even if these waiting periods are couple of minutes long, you can utilize them constructively. Imagine pooling 7 or 8 waiting periods of 2 minutes each in the course of a day and thereby saving 15 minutes every day.

At the end of the year, it will add up to a whopping 90 hours. You have just extended your life by 90 hours in a single year! So much can be accomplished in these extra reclaimed hours.

While A Phone Rings...Or In The Loo or Shower

A person learned 3 languages in his life time by reading vocabulary cards while peeing. A person spends several minutes a day discharging this bodily function. There is nothing much one can do in the loo anyway.

Another person learned 2 new skills while waiting for his phone to be answered. Average time is close to 10 seconds before a call gets answered. Several minutes a day can be saved by keeping some information cards in the pocket which can be leafed through during this period.

While taking shower, you can listen to some audio book and improve your knowledge. One person read over 50 books in 3 years while waiting for websites to load in computer. Of course this was way back when internet was slow. But still it is slow in many countries.

With the available technology, you can carry your office and library in your notebook computer or Ipad. A whole world has moved inside these electronic devices.

Earlier the witches used to see the world in their glass sphere but today we all are blessed with this privilege.

If you not so tech savvy, a small paperback book will fit easily into most women's purses and most men's briefcases. Bring one that is easy reading so that it won't require uninterrupted concentration.

Using Waiting Room or Commute As Your Workplace

We all have experienced the frustration of wasting time sitting in a waiting room, whether it be for a medical consultation or an interview. Whether you wait ten minutes for your own appointment or put in an hour of waiting room time, you know how tedious waiting can be. Instead of simply throwing that waiting room time away it is possible to use waiting room time productively. You can also put even ten minutes of waiting room time into some productive pursuit if you plan your activity ahead of time. This also applies to time spent in commuting or at an airport.

Read Something Worthwhile - If you know in advance that you will be stuck in a waiting room for more than five or ten minutes you can take advantage of the break in your day to do the reading you enjoy but seldom have time for.

Both by rising and by setting, the sun decreases the duration of life of everyone, except one who utilizes the time by discussing topics of the all-good Personality of Godhead.

This verse indirectly confirms the greater importance of utilizing the human form of life to realize our lost relationship with the Supreme Lord by acceleration of devotional service. Time and tide wait for no man. So the time indicated by the sunrise and the sunset will be uselessly wasted if such time is not properly utilized for realizing identification of spiritual values. Even a fraction of the duration of life wasted cannot be compensated by any amount of gold.

~ Srila Prabhupada (Srimad Bhagavatam 2.3.17)

Instead of sitting in frustration in the waiting room with magazines in which you have no interest, you can choose reading material in advance and bring it along.

This productive use of waiting room time can be enhanced by choosing your seat in the waiting room with care. Avoid sitting near the door or the check in area may prove too disruptive and make it difficult for you to concentrate.

Short Correspondence - Writing short letters in the waiting room especially when waiting for someone else, can be ideal because there are so few "at home" distractions. You can't wander out to the kitchen for a snack and there is no one with whom to chat. It's just you, the pen and the stationery you have brought with you. You will be able to check off an item that has been sitting for a long time on your to do list.

Short Walks - Technically this is an activity not done in the waiting room, but rather an activity that you can do once you realize you don't have to actually stay in a waiting room to be waiting. You can use your waiting room time productively by turning it into a 10, 15 even 20 minute walk that you know you need. Many buildings are comprised of long intersecting corridors that allow you to move at a comfortable exercise pace. If you are in a small office building with quick access to the outdoors you might even opt for a turn around the parking lot.

Handcrafts - When the amount of waiting room time is uncertain, you may choose to bring along a small ongoing craft project. Knitting, crocheting, needle point anything that can fit conveniently into a small, unobtrusive carry case can be used. This

---

I was once stuck in an airport with a long layover + a delayed flight and I started walking aimlessly in total frustration. And there, in a quiet corner of the airport, I saw a lady doing stretching exercises. She looked calm, serene and downright inspiring! So, depending on where you are this is definitely something to keep in mind.
~ Sumitha

kind of project will fill waiting room time productively and tends to occupy both the mind and the hands.

Make Lists or Write Notes - If you are really interested in making productive use of time spent in waiting rooms you should start to routinely carry a small, pocket note book and a pen. With this very basic equipment you can be ready to make productive use out of even the shortest waiting room stays. With pen, notebook and even five minutes you can easily create one of the many lists that can help you to better organize the following hour, day, week, month or beyond. Also you can organize your ideas or write an article even.

Lift Someone's Spirits - Often while spending time in a waiting room you cannot help but overhear the problems or the anxiety that someone else is experiencing. You can put your waiting room time to productive use by gently offering encouragement or simple distraction for the distraught patient.

Pray, Reflect or Meditate - Typically people go to a church, a temple or the silence of their favorite room when they want to pray, reflect or meditate. But the truth is that you really can pray, reflect or meditate almost anywhere and at any time if you put your mind to it. The key to using waiting room time productively to pray, reflect or meditate is to find that quiet zone in the waiting space that you have to use. Once you find that spot open up your prayerbook, take out a small photo that you might use for reflection or simply close your eyes to help block out distractions and center yourself on God. The peacefulness and relaxation induced by prayer, reflection or meditation gives the time you have spent in a waiting a value it otherwise would never have delivered.

Count Your Blessings - We get so carried away in the daily grind, that we hardly take the time to count our blessings. This can be a great time to think of all that is good in your life and send silent prayers for everyone (including God) who helped make it happen.

References

Nora Beane, Yahoo Contributor Network, Aug 8, 2006

Sumitha, AFineParent.com, February 4, 2013

Getting Things Done

The Art of Stress-Free Productivity

Getting Things Done is a time-management method, described in a book of the same title by productivity consultant David Allen. It is often referred to as GTD.

The GTD method rests on the idea of moving planned tasks and projects out of the mind by recording them externally and then breaking them into actionable work items. This allows one to focus attention on taking action on tasks, instead of on recalling them.

Methodology

In time management, task priorities play a central role. Allen's approach uses two key elements — control and perspective. He proposes a workflow process to control all the tasks and commitments that one needs or wants to get done. There are six "horizons of focus" to provide a useful perspective.

Allen creates analogies between the six levels of focus and an airplane taking off, going to higher altitudes:

Runway
10,000 feet level
20,000 feet level
30,000 feet level
40,000 feet level

50,000 feet level

Unlike some theories, which focus on top-down goal-setting, GTD works in the opposite direction. Allen argues that it is often difficult for individuals to focus on big picture goals if they cannot sufficiently control the day-to-day tasks that they frequently must face. By developing a system that clarifies and defines the regular workday, an individual can free up mental space to begin moving up to the next level of focus.

A weekly review is done on different levels, and suggests that the perspective gained from these reviews should drive one's priorities. This in turn determines the priority of the individual tasks and commitments gathered during the workflow process.

During a weekly review, determine the context for the tasks and put them on the appropriate lists. An example of grouping together similar tasks would be making a list of outstanding telephone calls, or the tasks / errands to perform while downtown. Context lists can be defined by the set of tools available or by the presence of individuals or groups for whom one has items to discuss or present.

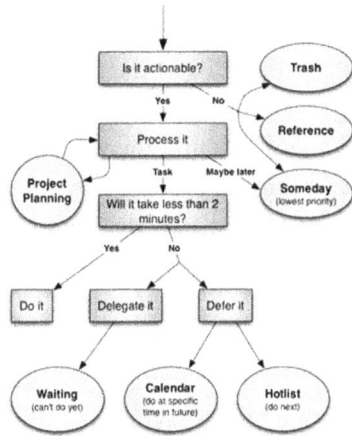

GTD is based on storing, tracking and retrieving the information related to the things that need to get done. Mental blocks we encounter are caused by insufficient 'front-end' planning. This means thinking in advance, generating a series of actions which can later be undertaken without further planning.

The human brain's "reminder system" is inefficient and seldom reminds us of what we need to do at the time and place when we can do it. Consequently, the "next actions" stored by context in the "trusted system" act as an external support which ensures that we are presented with the right reminders at the right time. As GTD relies on external memories, it can be seen as an application of the theories of distributed cognition or the extended mind.

Reception

In 2005, Wired called GTD "A new cult for the info age", describing the enthusiasm for this methodology among information technology and knowledge workers as a kind of cult following.

In 2005, Ben Hammersley interviewed David Allen for The Guardian article titled "Meet the man who can bring order to your universe", saying: "For me, as with the hundreds of thousands around the world who press the book into their friends' hands with fire in their eyes, Allen's ideas are nothing short of life-changing".

In 2007, Time Magazine called Getting Things Done the self-help business book of its time.

In 2007, Wired ran another article about GTD and Allen, quoting him as saying "the workings of an automatic transmission are more complicated than a manual transmission... to simplify a complex event, you need a complex system".

Software Implementations

While GTD material is technologically neutral and advises people to start with a paper-based system, many task management tools claim to implement GTD methodology.

The following software applications are designed for this purpose.
Proprietary
Binfire
DejaOffice
Evernote (The Secret Weapon)
Nirvana
Open Source
BasKet Note Pads

Chandler
Getting Things GNOME!

References:

Heylighen, Francis; Vidal, Clément (December 2008). "Getting Things Done: The Science behind Stress-Free Productivity". Long Range Planning: International Journal of Strategic Management 41 (6): 585–605. doi:10.1016/j.lrp.2008.09.004. ISSN 0024-6301.

Andrews, Robert (2005-07-12). "A new cult for the info age". Wired.com (Condé Nast). 2010-03-05.

Mann, Merlin (2004-09-08). "Getting started with "Getting Things Done"". 43 Folders. 2010-03-05.

Robinson, Keith (2006-03-21). "Best of GTD". Lifehacker. 2010-03-05.

"Review: Getting Things Done". The Simple Dollar. 2007-05-06. 2010-03-05.

Hammersley, Ben (2005-09-28). "Meet the man who can bring order to your universe". The Guardian (London: Guardian News and Media Limited). 2010-03-05.

Depending on God So Much

With So Little Time For Him

We try to keep God in church on Sunday morning...
	Maybe, Sunday night...
And, the unlikely event of a midweek service.
We do like to have Him around during sickness....
And, of course, at funerals.
However, we don't have time, or room, for Him during work or play...
Because.. That's the part of our lives we think... We can, and should, handle on our own.
May God forgive me for ever thinking...
That... There is a time or place where He is not to be first in my life.
Banishing God from places other than church, mosque or temple has caused a lot of problems in our world today. Respective followers of God confine themselves to their respective places of worship without feeling His presence in the creation or all living beings. God consciousness is meant to unite all living beings on a common platform, not divide them into factions and denominations.

Efficacy of Prayer

The efficacy of prayer has been the topic of various scientific studies since Francis Galton first addressed it in 1872. According to the Washington Post, "...prayer is the most common complement to mainstream medicine, far outpacing acupuncture, herbs, vitamins and other alternative remedies."

Prayer Reduces Stress

Social interactions are associated with positive health outcomes such as higher ratings of life-satisfaction, reduced risk of mortality, and decreased cardiovascular responses.

Similarly, religiosity has been found to be beneficial to both physical and mental health. Specifically, religious involvement has been associated with decreased blood pressure and heart rate.

Actually, luxury means nature's supply. You can have profuse supply of milk, grains. For dressing you can have profuse supply of silk, cotton. And for eating, profuse supply of grains, fruits, flowers. And for this profuse supply these are the means. The first thing is nadyah, rivers. The stock of water is the ocean, and by evaporation, cloud is formed. Just like you pump water to the topmost floor. So Krsna's pumping process is this cloud. Pumping process. He is, I mean to say, evaporating water throughout the whole summer season. And then through the clouds, the water is distributed all over the land. Parjanyah. Kamam vavarsa parjanyah [SB 1.10.4]. Because water is required. Just see how nice arrangement. And the water, whatever for the time being in the rainy season, is distributed. And for future supply it is stocked on top of the hills and mountains in the form of ice. And from those hills and mountains the rivers -- they are supposed to be water supply source -- throughout the year will supply water. It is stocked on the top. The same principle. We simply imitate. We also keep a very big tank on the rooftop of the house, and through pipe we get water supply. So here nature's pipe water supply is the big, big rivers.

~ Srila Prabhupada (Srimad-Bhagavatam 1.10.5 -- London, August 28, 1973)

Dr. Carl Jung, one of the greatest psychiatrists, says, "During the past thirty years, people from all the civilized countries of the earth have consulted me. I have treated many hundreds of patients. Among all my patients in second half of life – that is to say, over thirty five – there has not been one whose problem in the last resort was not that of finding a religious outlook on life. It is safe to say that every one of them fell ill because he had lost that which the living religion of every age have given to their followers, and none of them has been really healed who did not regain his religious outlook." (From 'Modern Man in Search of A Soul')

Mahatma Gandhi says in his book, 'My Experiment with Truth': "Without prayer, I should have been a lunatic long ago."

Time Management

Different Perspectives

A corporate executive, on holiday in a small, Greek sea-coast village, was strolling by the docks and taking in the local colour. He complimented one fisherman on the quality of his catch.

"How long did it take you to get all those fish?" he asked.

"Not very long," answered the Greek. "An hour or two."

"Then why didn't you stay out longer to catch more?"

Shrugging, the Greek explained that his catch was sufficient to meet his needs, and those of his family.

The executive asked, "But what do you do with the rest of your time?"

I sleep late, fish a little, play with my children, and take a nap with my wife. In the evening, I go to the village to see my friends, dance a little, play the bouzouki, and sing songs."

The executive said, "Well I have an MBA from Harvard and I'm sure I can help you. You should start by fishing longer every day. You'll catch extra fish that you can sell. With the revenue, you can buy a bigger boat. With the extra money the larger boat will bring you, you can buy a second boat and a third one, and so on, until you have an entire fleet of trawlers. Instead of selling your fish to a middleman, you can then negotiate directly with the processing plants and maybe even open your own plant.

You can ship fish to markets all around the world. In time, you can then move to New York City to direct your huge enterprise."

"How long would that take?" asked the Greek.

"Twenty, perhaps twenty-five years," replied the executive.

"And after that?"

"When your business gets really big, you can sell stock and make millions!" exclaimed the executive with zeal.

"Millions? Really? And after that?"

"After that you'll be able to retire, live in a small village near the coast, sleep late, play with your grandchildren, catch a few fish, take a nap with your wife, and spend your evenings singing, dancing, and playing the bouzouki with your friends."

So karmis are like that. He will eat two chapatis or four chapatis, but he is working day and night. If you want to see him, he will say, "Oh, I have no time." He does not think at any time that "I am interested to eat four chapatis, which can be very easily available. So why I am working so hard?" But that sense does not come. He is working, working, working, "More money, more money, more money, more money, more money." The Bhagavata says, "No, no. This is not your business." The four chapātis are already destined to you; you will get, any circumstances. You don't waste your time simply under some false impression of economic development. Don't waste your time. You cannot get more, you cannot get less. That is already there. So you utilize your time for understanding Krsna. That is your business. People will not accept it. "Oh, this is a waste of time. Attending the class of Bhagavad-gita, this is waste of time. By this time I could have earned hundreds of dollars." That is their business. That is called durbuddhi.
~ Srila Prabhupada (Bhagavad-gita 1.23 -- London, July 19, 1973)

Punctuality

Why Time Doesn't Fly At The Same Speed Around The Globe

Punctuality is the characteristic of being able to complete a required task or fulfill an obligation before or at a previously designated time. "Punctual" is often used synonymously with "on time".

According to each culture, there is often an understanding about what is considered an acceptable degree of punctuality. Usually, a small amount of lateness is acceptable; this is commonly about ten or fifteen minutes in Western cultures, but this is not the case in such instances as doctor's appointments or school lessons. In some cultures, such as Japanese society, or in the military, there basically is no allowance.

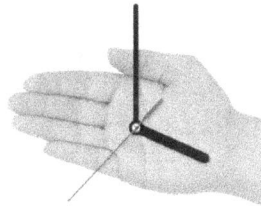

Some cultures have an unspoken understanding that actual deadlines are different from stated deadlines; for example, it may be understood in a particular culture that people will turn up an hour later than advertised. In this case, since everyone understands that a 9 am meeting will actually start around 10 am, no one is inconvenienced when everyone turns up at 10 am.

In cultures which value punctuality, being late is tantamount to showing disrespect for other's time and may be considered insulting. In such cases, punctuality may be enforced by social penalties, for example by excluding latecomers from meetings entirely.

Some Cultures Are Wound Tighter Than Others

Knowing a little about the culture can prevent much of the frustration.

Lateness is fashionable in one place, rude in another. Don't believe it? Try arriving early for dinner in Mexico.

In Switzerland, the land of watches, trains really do run like clockwork. If a commuter is 30 seconds late, the train is gone.

Step across the border, and you're in a different universe.

Italy has two rail schedules: the one printed in the brochure and another, flashing updates, on a board in the station. The first may be a fantasy; the second, reality.

Next to posted departures, "invariably you see the word 'ritardato' [delayed].

Your time or my time? When traveling, you're in 'their' time. And that can affect almost everything: catching trains and buses, shopping, getting a meal and making appointments.

It's important to go with the flow. If you go to a restaurant in Spain at 7 p.m., that's bad news. The staff is eating then.

Try going after 9 p.m., as the Spaniards do. For the Swiss, the earlier the better, say 6 p.m.; after 10, a tourist hoping for a hot meal in Switzerland just might go hungry.

As for the French, they are born with clocks in their stomachs. A wine merchant near Bordeaux is said to have halted in mid-sentence to break for lunch. In France, the lunch hour is sacred and it's not a short lunch.

By contrast, in some Latin American and southern European nations, hours and minutes seem hardly to matter.

In Mexico, guests invited to a 6 p.m. social dinner think nothing of showing up two or three hours later. In fact, it's wise to arrive at least an hour late for dinner in Mexico City to avoid embarrassing an unprepared host.

For Greeks, time can be as malleable as Dali's famous melting watches.

Theories abound as to why time doesn't fly at the same speed around the globe. Climate, economics and culture may play a role.

As you get closer to the equator, the pace of life seems to slow down. That might explain the familiar north-versus-south divisions within Europe, the Western Hemisphere and even within countries. Who cares to race the clock in 100-degree heat?

Some economists find truth in the saying "Money is time; time is money." Under this theory, rich societies move rapidly; poor societies poke along.

"Low-income countries have cultures, in general, in which the value of time is relatively low. In places where economic opportunities are limited, it's easier to give up an hour of work for leisure" -- or waiting.

Russia, where the popularity of punctuality grows as private enterprise expands, lends credence to this theory. In the past, they were working for the state and the waiting didn't come out of their pocketbook. Now a lot of people are working for themselves, and the norms are stricter.

The most intriguing ideas about how we treat time delve deeply into culture.

Of course, in every society, some people are punctual, some not. Culture just tips the balance.

A journalist assigned to Mexico City observed: Many Mexicans start the day with good intentions, trying to keep appointments.

But as they meet up with friends and acquaintances, a short "hello" won't do, and the minutes slip away.

Reference:

Jane Engle, Times, December 11, 2005

"Punctual - Definition and More from the Free Merriam-Webster Dictionary". Merriam-webster.com. 2012-08-31. 2014-02-01.

"Punctuality: Some cultures are wound tighter than others - Los Angeles Times". Articles. latimes.com. 1994-12-30. 2014-02-01.

"Germans and punctuality | All about those Germans | DW.DE | 09.12.2012". DW.DE. 2014-02-01.

White, Lawrence T. (2012-02-23). "Is "Punctuality Standard" an Oxymoron?". Psychology Today. 2014-02-01.

"Africa | Can Africa keep time?". BBC News. 2003-10-28. 2014-02-01.

Cultures

Monochronic or Polychronic

In his classic 1983 study, "The Dance of Life: The Other Dimension of Time," anthropologist Edward T. Hall used the words "monochronic" and "polychronic" to describe how different societies view time.

People in monochronic cultures, such as America and northern Europe, are task-oriented, Hall wrote. They do things in order, one at a time, starting with the most important and ending with the least.

Polychronic cultures, found in Mediterranean and many Latin American nations, he said, are "oriented toward people, human relationships and the family, which is the core of their existence." In this world, following a schedule is far less important than catching up with friends and family.

Monochronic Time

A monochronic time system means that things are done one at a time and time is segmented into precise, small units. Under this system time is scheduled, arranged and managed.

The United States is considered a monochronic society. This perception of time is learned and rooted in the Industrial Revolution, where "factory life required the labor force to be on hand and in place at an appointed hour" (Guerrero, DeVito & Hecht, 1999, p. 238).

For Americans, time is a precious resource not to be wasted or taken lightly. "We buy time, save time, spend time and make time. Our time can be broken down into years, months, days, hours, minutes, seconds and even milliseconds. We use time to structure both our daily lives and events that we are planning for the future. We have schedules that we must follow: appointments that we must go to at a certain time, classes that start and end at certain times, work schedules that start and end at certain times, and even our favorite TV shows, that start and end at a certain time."

As communication scholar Edward T. Hall wrote regarding the American's viewpoint of time in the business world, "the schedule is sacred." Hall says that for monochronic cultures, such as the American culture, "time is tangible" and viewed as a commodity where "time is money" or "time is wasted."

The result of this perspective is that Americans and other monochronic cultures, such as the German and Swiss, place a paramount value on schedules, tasks and "getting the job done." These cultures are committed to regimented schedules and may view those who do not subscribe to the same perception of time as disrespectful.

Monochronic cultures include Germany, the United Kingdom, Turkey, South Korea, Taiwan, Japan, Jamaica, Canada, Switzerland, most parts of the United States, and Scandinavia.

Polychronic Time

A polychronic time system is a system where several things can be done at once, and a more fluid approach is taken to scheduling time. Unlike most Americans and most northern and western European cultures, Latin American, African, Asian and Arab cultures use the polychronic system of time.

These cultures are much less focused on the preciseness of accounting for each and every moment.

As Raymond Cohen notes, polychronic cultures are deeply steeped in tradition and relationships rather than in tasks—a clear difference from their monochronic counterparts. Cohen notes that "Traditional societies have all the time in the world. The arbitrary divisions of the clock face have little saliency in cultures grounded in the cycle of the seasons, the invariant pattern of rural life, community life, and the calendar of religious festivities" (Cohen, 1997, p. 34).

Instead, their culture is more focused on relationships, rather than watching the clock. They have no problem being "late" for an event if they are with family or friends, because the relationship is what really matters.

As a result, polychronic cultures have a much less formal perception of time. They are not ruled by precise calendars and schedules. Rather, "cultures that use the polychronic time system often schedule multiple appointments simultaneously so keeping on schedule is an impossibility."

Polychronic cultures include Saudi Arabia, Egypt, China, Mexico, New Orleans, the Philippines, Pakistan, India, and many in Africa.

Predictable Patterns Between Cultures With Differing Time Systems

Monochronic People	Polychronic People
do one thing at a time	do many things at once
concentrate on the job	are highly distractible and subject to interruptions
take time commitments deadlines, schedules, seriously	consider an objective to be achieved, if possible
are low-context and need information	are high-context and already have information
committed to the job	are committed to people and human relationships

Monochronic People	Polychronic People
adhere religiously to plans	change plans often and easily
are concerned about not disturbing others; follow rules of privacy and consideration	are more concerned with those who are closely related than with privacy
show great respect for private property; seldom borrow or lend	borrow and lend things often and easily
emphasize promptness	base promptness on the relationship
are accustomed to short-term relationships	have strong tendency to build lifetime relationships

Co-Cultural Perspectives on Time

While the clash between the monochronic and polychronic perceptions of time can rifle the best of intentions in international settings, similar challenges can occur between co-cultures within an otherwise unified culture.

In the United States, the Hawaiian culture provides an example of how co-cultures can clash. Two time systems exist in Hawaii, where the Polynesians juggle two time systems: Haole time and Hawaiian time.

When you hear someone say "See you at two o'clock haole time," that means that they will see you at precisely two o'clock. But if you hear someone say, "I will be there at two o'clock Hawaiian time" then the message has an entirely different meaning. This is because Hawaiian time is very lax and basically means "when I get there."

Within the Native American community, the same relaxed concern for punctuality is dominant. Comments like "We're on Indian time, as usual" is commonly heard at many community events. Elders give calming reassurance that things "will happen when they happen" and "things happen when they are supposed to happen", implying there is a reason behind it all, even if it might not be apparent at the moment.

Moreover, it is common for individuals originating in India (a polychronic country) but inhabiting a monochronic environment like the U.S., to joke about their lax polychronic habits, saying "We follow DST: Desi Standard Time."

For a native of a monochronic country, this is nothing short of a nightmare, unless you are William Jefferson Clinton, the U.S. president (1992-2000) whose polychronic tendencies resulted in his aides' referring to items on his schedule as being in "Clinton Standard Time".

In some cultures, people place a high value on time and use time as a basis for decisions. In other cultures, time is less significant. For example, in Mexico or Central America tour guides may fail to indicate the correct arrival and departure times. In other countries, such as Switzerland, a traveler can set his or her watch by the promptness of the trains. When these cultures cross, expectancy with respect to time is violated and can cause discord between the people involved.

References:

Jane Engle, Times, December 11, 2005

Wikipedia

Adler, R.B., Lawrence B.R., & Towne, N. (1995). Interplay (6th ed.). Fort Worth: Hardcourt Brace College.

Ballard, D & Seibold, D., Communication-related organizational structures and work group temporal differences: the effects of coordination method, technology type, and feedback cycle on members' construals and enactments of time. Communication Monographs, Vol. 71, No. 1, March 2004, pp. 1–27

Buller D.B., & Burgoon, J.K. (1996). Interpersonal deception theory. Communication Theory, 6, 203-242.

Buller, D.B., Burgoon, J.K., & Woodall, W.G. (1996). Nonverbal communications: The unspoken dialogue (2nd ed.). New York: McGraw-Hill.

Burgoon, J.K., Stern, L.A., & Dillman, L. (1995). Interpersonal adaptation: Dyadic interaction patterns. Massachusetts: Cambridge University Press.

Eddelman, R.J., and Iwawaki, S. (1987). Self-reported expression and the consequences of embarrassment in the United Kingdom and Japan. Psychologia, 30, 205-216

Griffin, E. (2000). A first look at communication theory (4th ed). Boston, MA: McGraw Hill.

Gonzalez, G., & Zimbardo, P. (1985). Time in perspective. Psychology Today Magazine, 20-26.

Guerrero, L.K., Devito J.A.,& Hecht M.L. (1999). The Nonverbal Communication Reader: Classic and contemporary readings (2nd ed.). Long Grove, IL: Waveland Press, Inc.

Hall, E.T. & Hall, M. R. (1990). Understanding cultural differences: Germans, French, and Americans. Boston, MA: Intercultural Press.

African time

Emotional Time Consciousness vs Mechanical Time Consciousness

African time (or Africa time) is the perceived cultural tendency, in most parts of Africa, toward a more relaxed attitude to time. This is sometimes used in a pejorative sense, about tardiness in appointments, meetings and events. This also includes the more leisurely, relaxed, and less rigorously-scheduled lifestyle found in African countries, especially as opposed to the more clock-bound pace of daily life in Western countries. As such it is similar to time orientations in some other non-Western culture regions.

The appearance of a simple lack of punctuality or a lax attitude about time in Africa, may instead reflect a different approach and method in managing tasks, events, and interactions. Personal interactions and relationships are also managed in this way, such that it is not uncommon to have more than one simultaneous conversation. An African "emotional time consciousness" has been suggested which contrasts with Western "mechanical time consciousness".

My old finance lecturer, a Tanzanian with a wicked sense of humour, once told us this joke in class. "When God made man," he said, "He gave white man the watch, but he gave black man time!"
~ Nick, South Africa

Reactions To Time Orientation In Africa

Self-criticism

The concept of African time has become a key topic of self-criticism in modern Africa. According to one Ghanaian writer,

"One of the main reasons for the continuing underdevelopment of our country is our nonchalant attitude to time and the need for punctuality in all aspects of life. The problem of punctuality has become

Are Africans guilty of killing time?

English playwright, William Shakespeare, once said better three hours too soon than a minute late.

Well, in Africa, attitude to time-keeping is often the opposite of that.

Last week for instance, international journalists in the UK were kept waiting by the king of Ghana's largest ethnic group who was visiting Alexandra Palace in north London at the climax of a Ghanaian trade exhibition, Ghana Expo 2003.

The journalists had been informed that Otumfuo Osei Tutu II from the Ashanti would arrive at the exhibition at 1100.

The time was changed to 1400, but the king did not show up until two hours later when the journalists had already packed and left.

The incident only helped reinforce the belief held by many people in the developed world that Africans are terrible time-keepers.

Cases of a government minister keeping members of the public waiting, a friend turning up late for a date, a judge holding up court proceedings or a public service vehicle leaving and arriving late have become the norm rather than the exception.

~ BBC News, 28 October, 2003

so endemic that lateness to any function is accepted and explained off as 'African time.'"

In October 2007, an Ivorian campaign against African time, backed by President Laurent Gbagbo, received international media attention when an event called "Punctuality Night" was held in Abidjan to recognize business people and government workers for regularly being on time. The slogan of the campaign is "'African time' is killing Africa – let's fight it."

Reuters reported that "organizers hope to heighten awareness of how missed appointments, meetings or even late buses cut productivity in a region where languid tardiness is the norm."

Increasing foreign investments and international trade mean that Africans must realize promptness does not only define their future but also shows integrity.

The disparity in time awareness has seen international companies operating in the continent avoid employing local workers.

Some Chinese firms, for example, have opted to ship in staff from their home country. This move has inhibited their further integration into the local culture. It has also failed to create jobs for the local communities.

In nations where workers are locals, some firms have launched a master plan, known as the "Mr White Man's Time," that seeks to influence Africans' punctuality at work.

Calls for the continent to change its way of life, however, continue to be met with some hostility. This is because it is still perceived as "un-African" to be punctual.

Africans claim it is a Western obsession with efficiency, which must not be forced down their throats. They see no wrong with their "timing challenges."

Indeed, Africans claim even the employment of a "red-hot stove" approach will not arrest the said attitude. In most parts of Gambia, Ethiopia, remote villages in Kenya and the Democratic Republic of Congo, among other countries, time is figured out without a watch. They take into account the movement of the sun and prayer times.

~ Global Times | Mark Kapchanga, June 13, 2013

It was remarked that this year's winner, legal adviser Narcisse Aka—who received a $60,000 villa in recognition of his punctuality—"is so unusually good at being punctual that his colleagues call him 'Mr White Man's Time'".

Popular culture

The contrast between African time and Western time is illustrated in the award-winning short film Binta and the Great Idea. The protagonist of the film, a fisherman in a small village in Senegal, can't understand the new ideas brought back from Europe by his friend; these are symbolized by a Swiss wristwatch, which rings at various times to the delight of the friend, but for no apparent reason. The fisherman is shown making his way through the various ranks of officials with his idea, which in the end is a sharp criticism of Western culture's obsession with efficiency and progress.

References

"What is this thing called African Time?". Daily Maverick. 2010-01-21. 2014-04-01.

"Time for Africa to abandon tardy culture to avoid punctuality problems - OP-ED". Globaltimes.cn. 2013-06-13. 2014-02-01.

By Josh Macabuag. "Adjusting to Africa time - CNN.com". edition.cnn.com. 2014-03-16.

"Can Africa keep time?". BBC News. 28 October 2003. 2008-02-18.

"Backdrop of poverty to a wealth of nations". The Daily Telegraph. August 26, 2002. 2008-02-18.

http://ijbssnet.com/journals/Vol_3_No_11_June_2012/5.pdf

"International Community Resources: Cultural Differences," Iowa State University, accessed 2010-1-30]

Solomon, Charlene, and Michael S. Schellalse. 2009. Managing Across Cultures: The 7 Keys to Doing Business with a Global Mindset, p. 174, accessed 2010-1-30

'Take Your Time'

Ikaria, Greece

As we have seen already, culture plays an important role in one's perception of time, priorities, and deadlines.

Values-based time management means making choices on what projects/tasks are important. But what is important to one person may be unimportant to somebody else, and is affected by one's principles and values, traditions and group norms, work ethic, and other factors. For example, there is so-called 'Brazilian' or 'Filipino' time vs. precise 'Swiss' time. Then there is this 'Ikaria' time, within the overall 'Greece time'.

Ikaria seems to laugh in the face of modern life- the greedy rush through time, the loss of identity through globalization and homogenous life styles, consumerism, materialism and an official, or unofficial police state that observes and dictates the rules of living where there is meant to be freedom.

Its not only Africa. My wife went to a wedding in Portugal earlier this year and the priest turned up an hour late. The Portuguese people there did not seem at all concerned, apparently this is normal for that country. Perhaps the question we should really be asking is, are North Europeans and Americans too "up tight" about time keeping?

~ Scott, Los Angeles

Hidden somewhere on this remote, mountainous Greek island, may be the answer to one of life's most enduring questions: How can we live longer, healthier lives?

Ikarians are an impressively self-sufficient people, mainly shepards who own goats in the thousands. They farm their own land - with most households tending their own supply of organic fruit, vegetables and herbs. Some others are shop or taverna owners. Youths start learning to tend the land and herd goats, as well as other traditional labour, as early as their adolescent years.

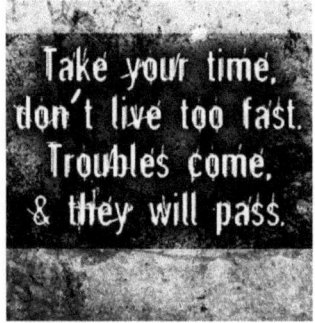

Take your time, don't live too fast. Troubles come, & they will pass.

Towns here exist beyond the normal confines of time. In all Ikaria, the people live exclusively at their own pace; if a shop owner feels like opening his store at 18:00, so be it. After all, the mentality goes, it's their life, and their store, and there is no need to live life throttled by some artificial social compulsion.

These inhabitants live on average 10 years longer than the rest of Western Europe. Six out of 10 of people aged over 90 are still

> *Sometimes people misunderstand, thinking that sages who try for self-realization are lazy. In a high-court a judge is sitting soberly, apparently doing nothing, and he is getting the highest salary. And another man in the same court -- he's working hard all day long, rubber-stamping, and he is getting not even one-tenth of the judge's salary. He's thinking, "I am so busy and working so hard, yet I am not getting a good salary. And this man is just sitting on the bench, and he's getting such a fat salary." The criticism of Hinduism as "inhibiting progress" is like that: it comes out of ignorance. The Vedic civilization is for self-realization. It is meant for the intelligent person, the person who will not just work like an ass but who will try for that thing which he did not achieve in so many other lives -- namely, self-realization.*
> *~ Srila Prabhupada (Civilization and Transcendence 2, Progressing Beyond "Progress")*

physically active. Experts says only about 20 percent of how long we live is dictated by genes; the rest is lifestyle.

Wake up naturally, work in the garden, have a late lunch, take a nap. One cherished custom of Ikarians is the mid-day siesta or afternoon nap. You walk in one of these villages in mid-afternoon and it's like a ghost town. People are taking their naps and it's said that taking a 30-minute nap at least five times per week decreases the chance of heart attack by one-third. It also reduces stress and makes you look and feel younger.

People here have a low sense of time urgency. Take your time - is a popular slogan here.

When you ask people what time it is they say "late thirty." When you invite somebody to come to lunch you don't say come at noon you say come on Thursday and they may come any time between ten in the morning and six in the evening.

There is very little stress of any kind. People don't wear watches in Ikaria. Showing up late is socially accepted. This attitude reduces stress and wrinkles. They seem to prefer owning rather than being owned by time.

Punctuality in Japan

On the night that Shinji and Hatsue, 2 lovers agree to meet at the top of the village steps, Shinji leaves his home two hours early. He positions himself at Yashiro Shrine, only steps away from the meeting point. As the time nears, Shinji counts the eleven strokes of the clock. At that instant, he moves to the top of the stairs in anticipation of Hatsue. If Shinji had come even one minute late, Hatsue might have been offended. Japanese culture emphasizes punctuality and deadlines.

What Americans consider being "fashionably late," Japanese consider rebellious and egocentric. Punctuality governs social interactions and preserves group harmony. Without exception, individuals expect others to be on time. A recent Tokyo survey reported that in Japan only five percent of women and four percent of men have wristwatches that are set inaccurately.

Researchers Robert Levine and Ellen Wolff rank Japan as the country with the best "punctuality concept." Survey results indicate that Japanese college students are late to class less than once per week, and teachers punish lateness by lowering grades. Even among close friends or lovers, like Hatsue and Shinji, lateness is an insult in social settings. Punctuality dominates many facets of Japanese life. Average walking speed, accuracy of bank clocks, and post office efficiency are the highest in the world. In business, although deadlines are important, they do not take precedence over relationship building.

Japanese deadlines are realistic because, once established, they are rarely broken. They allow people enough time to build solid relationships and reach consensus. During octopus season, the fishermen in the novel awaken at 2:30 or 3:00 in the morning, taking breakfast at a leisurely pace and allowing sufficient time to get to the shore. Lateness is seen as an insult to the boss, and, given the importance of relationships, it is something employees want to avoid. In the context of Japanese culture, Shinji's acute awareness of time is expected, even when meeting his lover.

Bibliography

Brake, Terrance, Danielle Medina Walker, and Thomas Walker. Doing Business Internationally. New York: Irwin, 1995.

Ellington, Lucien. Japan: A Global Studies Handbook. Santa Barbara: ABC-CLIO, 2002.

"Japanese Women May be More Punctual Than Men." Yahoo News. 17 Aug. 2002. 13 Oct. 2002.< http://in.news.yahoo.com/020817/64/1tvyj.html>.

Morrison, Terri, Wayne A. Conaway, and George A. Borden. Kiss, Bow, or Shake Hands. Holbrook: Adams, 1994.

Wing Chung, Rita. Punctuality. Spring 1999. ESL 1411. 13 Oct. 2002 <http://www.rescomp.wustl.edu/~kschwelle/wcrnE2.htm>.

Germans and punctuality

Germans are famously punctual, and proud of it. You can set your clocks by them. Admittedly, Germans didn't invent the clock, but they are trailblazers when it comes to making things as reliable as clockwork. If they weren't, disaster would surely strike. That's why trains, buses and planes are always on time on Germany.

They say that "punctuality is the politeness of kings." Fair enough. But that's not to say that Germans are punctual because they're royalists. They just are. German philosopher Immanuel Kant allegedly got up at 5 a.m. every morning, went to his university at 7 a.m., worked from 9 a.m. to 1 p.m. on his books, took a walk at 3.30 p.m. - seven times up and down the Lindenallee in the Prussian city of Königsberg, never more, never less - and went to bed at 10 p.m. sharp. Kant is the poster boy for German punctuality.

Better to be five minutes early than one minute late in Germany. It has to be said that not all Germans follow his example. But they try. Nearly 85 percent of Germans say they take their appointments seriously and expect others to do the same. In Germany, the rule of thumb is that it's better to be five minutes early than one minute late. There is a phrase - "pünktlich wie die Maurer" - punctual as the mason. Masons are especially punctual, at least when it comes to laying down their tools. It's said that they never work a second beyond their shift. Perhaps that's as much of a German tradition as punctuality.

On a Date

Germans are sometimes ridiculed and sometimes secretly admired for their obsessive timekeeping. Visitors report that they are neither early, nor late, but exactly on time.

They like to organise every llittle bit of their lives, leave nothing to chance. Many have the motto "Ordnung ist das halbe Leben", organisation is half of one's life (literally translated).

Being punctual is polite and shows respect.

And yet, one can have an appointment at clinic, and will wait and wait. The doctor takes his time, but the patient must be on time for the appointment.

When on a date, people drive around the block a few times so that they can arrive for the date at exactly the right time.

Jayant Thatte reports in Business Line:

"I was going to Berlin using car pooling in my first month in Deutschland and I was supposed to meet a gentleman at 8 am. Old habits die hard and I was a few minutes late. At 8:02 I got a call from him. He sounded worried and he asked me if there was any misunderstanding about the time or venue. I learnt that in Deutschland, 8 is not the same as 7:59 or 8:01."

"If a Deutsche-Bahn (one of the most efficient public transport networks in Europe) train is delayed by even five minutes, the train crew will apologise to the passengers for the delay."

Reference:

Peter Zudeick

Jayant Thatte, Business Line, January 20, 2013)

February 28

Dealing With Lateness

Solving Punctuality Problems

Punctuality is important for productivity and team morale. Do you have a colleague who regularly arrives late for meetings? It's an annoying habit, and it's even worse if everyone else must wait for him because he's a key person in the decision-making process.

Or perhaps you have a colleague who frequently turns up late at the office, complaining about "nightmare traffic" on her drive to work.

Worse still, are you the person who is always late?

Lateness is bad for team productivity or team morale, and it may point to a wider lack of responsibility. So, what can you do to stop it?

This article helps you understand how to stop persistent lateness – whether you're the guilty party, or it's a member of your team.

Understanding Lateness

Whoever the habitual latecomer is, identifying why the lateness occurs is the first step toward eliminating it. Sometimes the causes will be obvious. Other times, the reason for habitual lateness can be rooted in the person's subconscious.

Here are some common reasons for lateness:

1. Disorganization

People who are late due to disorganization simply lose track of time. They're not effective schedulers, or they're overly optimistic about what they can accomplish in a certain amount of time.

Disorganization can also be caused by an inability to say no to commitments. For instance, you might have said yes to that 10:00 meeting, but you really don't have time for it. You try to do everything on your morning schedule, but you're still late by 15 minutes.

Some people also subconsciously stay disorganized because they like the adrenaline rush – the "buzz" that comes with just hitting a deadline. Unfortunately, where people do this, the smallest delay can cause them to be late.

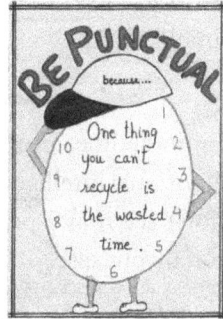

2. The Power Play

Using lateness as a "power play" is more common at work than in social settings, and it can become quite widespread in an organization's culture.

Sometimes people use lateness, especially when arriving at meetings, to show that they're more important or more powerful than everyone else. Waiting for someone is a subtle form of deference and respect for that person, and making others wait can give that person's ego a boost.

People may also use lateness to prove that they're busier than the rest of the team. They're so busy doing all of their work that they can't possibly show up on time!

3. Anxiety or Avoidance

People can be chronically late when they want to avoid certain situations. For instance, if you're managing someone who's always late to meetings, perhaps that person is being bullied by someone on the team. Or, perhaps that person is worried about his or her performance, or doesn't feel adequate in the position.

Because this person fears the situation so much, he or she may take as much time as possible to get there. The lateness means the person has to spend less time in that situation.

Or perhaps he or she resents the meeting and views it as a waste of time. Here, lateness is a "passive aggressive" way of registering an objection.

4. Poor Social Skills

Sometimes people are late because they simply don't have the emotional intelligence to see how their lateness affects others. They don't see it as a problem, so they think it must not be a problem for anyone else.

5. Medical Reasons

If you, or someone on your team, recently became a chronic latecomer, then this could be a sign of a much larger problem, like depression, chronic fatigue, or another illness.

How to Stop Lateness

So, how can you stop habitual lateness?

There are several strategies you can use. We'll break down each of them by cause, and we'll include tips if you're a manager of a habitual latecomer.

1. Disorganization

• Keep a schedule with you at all times. Write down every meeting or commitment you have. It also helps if you schedule travel or transition time to and from each meeting or commitment. Online schedulers are useful if you're always late, because a computer alarm can remind you when it's time to leave for a meeting or appointment.

• Stop procrastinating. Procrastination uses up your time, and it's a common cause for lateness. Promise yourself a small reward each time you show up promptly for a commitment.

• Put a "lateness buffer" into your schedule. For example, if a meeting starts at 9:30, put it on your schedule for 9:15. This extra 15 minutes will give you extra time to get where you're going.

For Managers

• Put the person's lateness into perspective. If he's 15 minutes late for a meeting with eight other people, then he just cost the company two hours' worth of work. Looking at lateness from this viewpoint can motivate the person to be on time. It's also helpful to put a monetary figure on this lost time.

2. The Power Play

• Look at this from the perspective of everyone who is waiting for you. Wouldn't you feel devalued or taken advantage of if you always had to wait for someone else? Is this really the image you want to present to your team?

• Analyze why you need to feel more important than others on your team. This can be an uncomfortable conversation to have with yourself, but it can be enlightening if you're willing to be honest. For instance, you could discover that you really have low self-esteem, and you therefore overcompensate by being late. If so, this may enable you to take steps to improve and grow.

Here is the written explanation you wanted for my coming late yesterday, sir!

• Arriving late to prove to others that you're more important is just bad behavior. Other team members may have to stay late to make up for the lost time they spent waiting for you. Would you want to be treated this way?

For Managers

• If you suspect that one of your team members arrives late as a power play, then have a sincere, but firm, talk with him. Let him know that you value all team members equally, and you don't appreciate him chronic lateness. If he continues the behavior, it might be time for disciplinary action.

• If you suspect that a team member is late to prove to you how busy he is, then acknowledge the good work he's doing and remind him that lateness wastes everyone's time, including yours.

• If a team member is consistently late for meetings (even if the meetings depend on his presence), then take control! Use effective meeting skills, and start without him. He'll get the message.

3. Anxiety or Avoidance

• If you're subconsciously arriving late to avoid a situation, then you must confront the situation, at least within yourself. If you feel that you can't handle your job or assignment, then take steps to improve your skills. This will give you more self-confidence and help you cope with your workload.

• If you avoid a situation due to someone else behaving unpleasantly, then raise the issue with him in a neutral zone. Be honest, but firm, about how he makes you feel. If his behavior persists, then it might be time to inform your boss.

• If you're late because you resent attending the meeting, perhaps because you consider it a waste of time, or perhaps because you're busy and you've got other things you need to focus on, then it's time to brush up on your assertiveness and negotiation skills. Talk with the leader of the meeting and see if you can stop attending, if you can shorten the meeting, or if you can limit your attendance to only one, short part of it.

For Managers

• If you suspect that someone on your team is late because he feels overwhelmed or inadequate in his position, then have a one-on-one talk with him. Offer him additional training or tools so he feels more prepared.

• If you suspect a bullying situation, then it's important to know for sure before taking action. Watch your team carefully. If you notice bullying, take action to stop it immediately. Bullying not only lowers morale, but hurts productivity and may increase absenteeism.

• If you suspect that someone is late because they don't want to attend, talk to them, and explore what they think. Where their attendance is necessary, explain the business reasons why this is the case. Where it is not, be open to allowing them to skip the meeting, or attend only part of it.

4. Poor Social Skills

• If you want to learn whether your lateness truly affects those around you, then ask. Your colleagues might not say what you want to hear, but these conversations can tell you a lot. Hearing how your lateness impacts others can be a powerful motivator for change.

For Managers

• Remind the person that his lateness makes others on the team, who did arrive on time, feel resentful and angry. His chronic lateness can really annoy others, and damage teamwork.

In Hrsikesh in 1977, Srila Prabhupada was staying with about eight of his disciples in a house on the bank of the Ganges. One day Prabhupada entered the kitchen and was astonished to see that the devotees had cut up a huge amount of vegetables in preparation for lunch. Prabhupada said they had cut enough vegetables to feed fifty people. Commenting that his disciples had no common sense, Prabhupada then sat in a chair and began directing them in all the details of the cooking. He watched the rice boiling and tested it for softness. Then he personally cooked the capatis. At this time, Prabhupada commented that only a lazy man cannot cook, and he told the story of some lazy men.

There was a king who announced that all lazy men in his kingdom could come to the charity house and be fed. Hundreds of people came and they all said, "I am a lazy man." The king then told his minister to set fire to the charity house. Everyone inside, except two men, immediately ran out of the burning building. Of the two remaining, one man said to the other, "My back is becoming very hot from the fire." The other man advised, "Just turn over to the other side." Seeing these two, the king said, "They are actually lazy men. Feed them."
~ Srila Prabhupada Nectar 2

5. Medical Reasons

• If you used to be punctual, but now you drag yourself to work late every day, then it's important to make sure there's no underlying medical issue. Have you been feeling especially tired or depressed? If so, then you should see your doctor.

• Try going to bed earlier and drinking more water. Lack of sleep and dehydration can cause feelings of fatigue and moodiness.

For Managers

• If you suspect medical issues, then try working with your team member. Can you give him time off to rest and recover?

The Urgent/Important Matrix

Using Time Effectively, Not Just Efficiently

Your boss has asked you to prepare an important presentation for the next board meeting. You only have a few days to put the presentation together, your workload is already high, and you have a number of other "urgent" tasks on your To-Do List. You're anxious, you can't concentrate, and everything seems to distract you.

Time stressors are the most pervasive source of pressure and stress in the workplace, and they happen as a result of having too much to do, in too little time. So, how can you beat this stress, and deliver the things that really matter to do a good job?

The Urgent/Important Matrix helps you think about your priorities, and determine which of your activities are important, and which are, essentially, distractions. In this article, we'll look at how you can use the Urgent/Important Matrix to manage your time effectively.

What Are "Urgent" and "Important" Activities?

Great time management means being effective as well as efficient. Managing time effectively, and achieving the things that you want to achieve, means spending your time on things that are important and not just urgent. To do this, and to minimize the stress of having too many tight deadlines, it's important to understand this distinction:

Important activities have an outcome that leads to the achievement of your goals, whether these are professional or personal.

Urgent activities demand immediate attention, and are often associated with the achievement of someone else's goals.

Urgent activities are often the ones we concentrate on; they demand attention because the consequences of not dealing with them are immediate.

Attribution

The idea of measuring and combining these two competing elements in a matrix has been attributed to both former US President Eisenhower and Dr Stephen Covey.

Eisenhower's quote, "What is important is seldom urgent and what is urgent is seldom important," sums up the concept of the matrix perfectly. This so-called "Eisenhower Principle" is said to be how Eisenhower organized his tasks. As a result, the matrix is sometimes called the Eisenhower Matrix.

Covey brought the idea into the mainstream and gave it the name "The Urgent/Important Matrix" in his 1994 business classic The 7 Habits of Highly Effective People.

How to Use the Tool

The Urgent/Important Matrix is a powerful way of thinking about priorities. Using it helps you overcome the natural tendency to focus on urgent activities, so that you can keep clear enough time to focus on what's really important. This is the way you move from "firefighting" into a position where you can grow your business and your career.

Here's how it works:

The matrix can be drawn with the dimensions of Importance and Urgency.

Follow the steps below to use the matrix to prioritize your activities:

The first step is to list all the activities and projects that you feel you have to do. Try to include everything that takes up your time at work, however unimportant. (If you manage your time using a To-Do List or Action Program, you should have done this already.)

Next, on a scale of 1 to 5, assign importance to each of the activities.

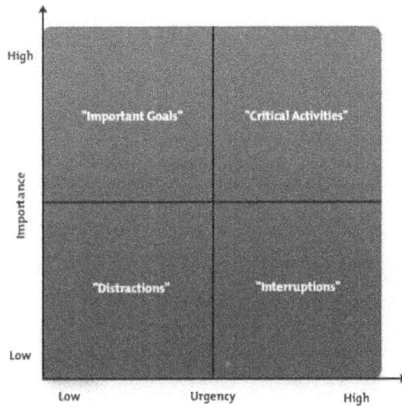

Remember, this is a measure of how important the activity is in helping you meet your goals and objectives. Try not to worry about urgency at this stage.

Once you've assigned an importance value to each activity, evaluate its urgency. As you do this, plot each item on the matrix according to the values that you've given it.

Now study the matrix using the strategies described below to schedule your priorities.

Strategies for Different Quadrants of the Matrix

Urgent and Important

There are two distinct types of urgent and important activities: Ones that you could not foresee, and others that you've left to the last minute.

You can avoid last-minute activities by planning ahead and avoiding procrastination.

Issues and crises, on the other hand, cannot always be foreseen or avoided. Here, the best approach is to leave some time in your schedule to handle unexpected issues and unplanned important activities. (If a major crisis arises, then you'll need to reschedule other events.)

If you have a lot of urgent and important activities, identify which of these could have been foreseen, and think about how you could schedule similar activities ahead of time, so that they don't become urgent.

Urgent and Not Important

Urgent but not important activities are things that stop you achieving your goals, and prevent you from completing your work. Ask yourself whether these tasks can be rescheduled, or whether you can delegate them.

A common source of such interruptions is from other people in your office. Sometimes it's appropriate to say "No" to people politely, or to encourage them to solve the problem themselves). Alternatively, try scheduling time when

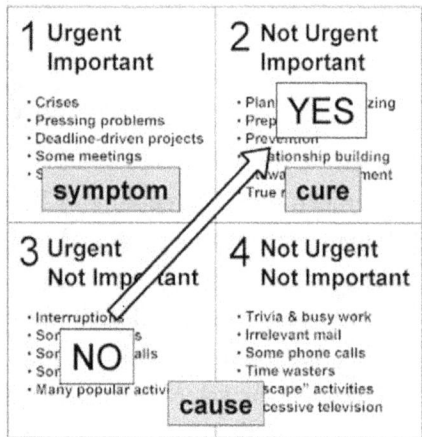

1 Urgent Important	2 Not Urgent Important
· Crises · Pressing problems · Deadline-driven projects · Some meetings · S... **symptom**	· Plan... **YES** zing · Prep... · Prevention ...tionship building ...wa... ...ment True r... **cure**
3 Urgent Not Important	4 Not Urgent Not Important
· Interruptions · Sor... s · Sor... **NO** alls · Sor... · Many popular activi...	· Trivia & busy work · Irrelevant mail · Some phone calls · Time wasters ...scape" activities **cause** ...cessive television

you are available, so that people know that they can interrupt you at these times (a good way of doing this is to schedule a regular meeting, so that all issues can be dealt with at the same time.) By doing this, you'll be able to concentrate on your important activities for longer periods of time.

Not Urgent, but Important

These are the activities that help you achieve your personal and professional goals, and complete important work. Make sure that you have plenty of time to do these things properly, so that they do not become urgent. And remember to leave enough time in your schedule to deal with unforeseen problems. This will maximize your chances of keeping on schedule, and help you avoid the stress of work becoming more urgent than necessary.

Not Urgent and Not Important

These activities are just a distraction, and should be avoided if possible. Some can simply be ignored or cancelled. Others are activities that other people may want you to do, but they do not contribute to your own desired outcomes. Again, say "No" politely, if you can.

If people see you are clear about your objectives and boundaries, they will often not ask you to do "not important" activities in the future.

Holy Grail Of Time Management

This method is regarded as the holy grail of time management. Therefore we will "repeat" these concepts once again as presented by Eisenhower for better understanding.

The Eisenhower Method

He was the American general (he later became president of the US) who invaded France when occupied by the Germans in the second world war. He commanded 2 million soldiers and was forced to find a better way to control them. He then came up with the Eisenhower method.

How To Use The Eisenhower Method

Using the Eisenhower quadrant is very easy. You pick an item from your Todo list and you ask yourself these two questions.

"Is it urgent?"

"Is it important?"

You can now put the action into the correct quadrant. Below is an explanation of each quadrant.

4. Not Urgent and Not Important

Examples:

Time wasters (Ex: Facebook, checking e-mails all the time...)

Busy work (Ex: Work that doesn't need to be done)

Procrastinating

You should not spend any time on activities in this quadrant. When is something not important? If it doesn't help you in any way to progress towards your goals. If it doesn't progress you toward your goals, then why should you spend time doing it?

When is something not urgent? If it doesn't matter when it is done, then it's not urgent. It can be done today, or it can be done next week or even next year, it doesn't matter.

The combination of not urgent and not important is the worst quadrant to spend your time in. Decrease your time in this quadrant and put it somewhere else. I prefer you put it in 'not urgent and important'.

3. Urgent and Not Important

Examples:

Answering e-mails

Incoming phone calls

Interrupting colleagues

I recommend not spending time here either. Since the tasks are still not important and you're still not progressing towards your goals. However, these tasks are urgent, therefore you can't schedule them. They're also hard to ignore, since urgent action are often in your face and demand attention. Ex: A phone call or an interrupting colleague.

You need to find a way to deal with these as quickly as possible. One way is to decrease the change of other people disturbing you. You can do this by putting up a busy sign on your door. Next, if they get past the busy sign, you need to handle their interruptions quickly. Say up front that you're very busy and ask them to state their business quickly. Their's no point in just sending them away, since they already succeeded in disturbing you. You might as well listen to their request and note it down. As soon as you know why they disturbed you, send them away to continue working on the important stuff.

Dealing with interruptions and distractions have been dealt with in the earlier volume.

2. Urgent and Important

Examples:
Emergencies (ex: Crying baby...)
Troubleshooting
Deadlines

You have to do these actions. They're important. They progress you toward your goals, however, since they're urgent, they're often unplanned and unwanted.

You will always spend some time here, since emergencies will always happen. When they do, you have to deal with them. No excuses. After you dealt with the situation, spend time to make sure it never

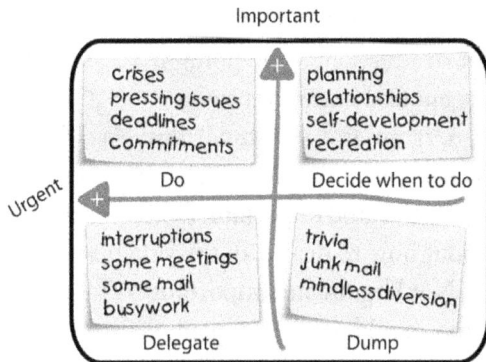

happens again or minimize it's occurrence or make preparations for when it happens again.

Ex: When cooking, make sure you have all the ingredients before starting, because you don't want to be running to the shop to buy some salt when you're in the process of cooking.

1. Not Urgent and Important

Examples:
Building quality relationships with other people
Doing actual work to progress toward a major goal
Physical exercise
Spiritual activities

This is the quadrant in which you should spent most of your time. Most people however, don't do this and spent most of their time in any of the other quadrants. Because these important tasks don't scream to you like a ringing phone, they're often neglected in favour of more urgent matters.

If you spend almost no time here, then your first important task is to save some time each day to work on the important things. One thing you can do, is to set up systems to avoid urgent tasks. For example, if you do a lot of troubleshooting on your project. Spend time to fix errors beforehand to decrease the time cleaning up after the errors.

Summary of the Eisenhower Method

Not urgent and not important: Don't do these, if you spend a lot of time here, stop doing it and start spending time in the 'not urgent and important' zone.

Urgent and not important: Avoid these as much as possible. When you're interrupted, handle it as fast as possible.

Urgent and important: Do these, when done, spend time to think about how to deal with the situation in the future.

Not Urgent and important: While not urgent, all your available time should go to this quadrant.

---

tasyaiva hetoh prayateta kovido
na labhyate yad bhramatam upary adhah
tal labhyate duhkhavad anyatah sukham
kalena sarvatra gabhira-ramhasa

Persons who are actually intelligent and philosophically inclined should endeavor only for that purposeful end which is not obtainable even by wandering from the topmost planet [Brahmaloka] down to the lowest planet [Patala]. As far as happiness derived from sense enjoyment is concerned, it can be obtained automatically in course of time, just as in course of time we obtain miseries even though we do not desire them.
~ Srila Prabhupada (Srimad Bhagavatam 1.5.18)

You can make a goal of spending at least 80% of your time in the 'Not urgent and important' quadrant. The other 20% will be divided between 'urgent and important' and 'urgent and not important'.

Always use the Eisenhower method when adding items to your Todo list. Always ask yourself whether it is important and whether it is urgent.

Reference

Demian, Fluent Time Management

Elisabeth Hendrickson. "The Tyranny of the "To Do" List". Sticky Minds. October 31, 2005. — an anecdotal discussion of how to-do lists can be tyrannical

Buck, M. L., Lee, M. D., MacDermid, S., & Smith S. C. (2000). Reduced load work and the experience of time among professionals and managers: Implications for personal and organizational life. In C. Cooper & D. Rousseau (Eds.), Trends in Organizational Behavior (Vol. 7). New York: John Wiley & Sons.

THE AUTHOR

Dr. Sahadeva dasa (Sanjay Shah) is a monk in vaisnava tradition. His areas of work include research in Vedic and contemporary thought, Corporate and educational training, social work and counselling, travelling, writing books and of course, practicing spiritual life and spreading awareness about the same.

He is also an accomplished musician, composer, singer, instruments player and sound engineer. He has more than a dozen albums to his credit so far. (SoulMelodies.com)

His varied interests include alternative holistic living, Vedic studies, social criticism, environment, linguistics, history, art & crafts, nature studies, web technologies etc.

Many of his books have been acclaimed internationally and translated in other languages.

By The Same Author

Oil-Final Countdown To A Global Crisis And Its Solutions

End of Modern Civilization And Alternative Future

To Kill Cow Means To End Human Civilization

Cow And Humanity - Made For Each Other

Cows Are Cool - Love 'Em!

Let's Be Friends - A Curious, Calm Cow

Wondrous Glories of Vraja

We Feel Just Like You Do

Tsunami Of Diseases Headed Our Way - Know Your Food Before Time Runs Out

Cow Killing And Beef Export - The Master Plan To Turn India Into A Desert
By 2050

Capitalism Communism And Cowism - A New Economics For The 21st Century

Noble Cow - Munching Grass, Looking Curious And Just Hanging Around

World - Through The Eyes Of Scriptures

To Save Time Is To Lengthen Life

An Inch of Time Can Not Be Bought With A Mile of Gold

Lost Time Is Never Found Again

Spare Us Some Carcasses - An Appeal From The Vultures

Cow Dung - A Down-To- Earth Solution To Global Warming And Climate
Change

Cow Dung For Food Security And Survival of Human Race

(More information on availability on DrDasa.com)

www.ingramcontent.com/pod-product-compliance
Lightning Source LLC
Chambersburg PA
CBHW070631030426
42337CB00020B/3976